LEGENDS OF A SKY MARSHALL

JERRY WORLEY

LEGENDS OF A SKY MARSHALL

Copyright © 2024 **Jerry Worley**

ISBN (Paperback): 978-1-964494-11-1
ISBN (Hardback): 978-1-964494-40-1
ISBN (Ebook): 978-1-964494-12-8

Printed in the United States of America.

PROMINENT
BOOKS
EDGE

5830 E 2nd St, Ste 7000 #9983
Casper, WY 82609
USA

Dedication

This reprint of the book I originally published in 2003 is dedicated to all those men and women who spent or are spending countless hours on flights around the world prepared to give their own lives to defend the aircraft and passengers from those who would seek to do them harm.

Only those who have performed these honorable duties will understand the hours of boredom anticipating the one moment when they are called into action. The country owes them a debt of gratitude since they are the last line of defense to prevent a repeat of the tragedy of 9/11 or some other horror being devised by those who desire to harm the United States.

Some of us sky marshals were pleased to be invited to the 50th Anniversary of the Federal Air Marshal program held at TSA offices around the country on March 2, 2012. The date stems from the 1961 decision by President Kennedy to arm a small number of FAA safety inspectors to deal with the hijacking of aircraft to Cuba. This was followed in 1970 with the decision of President Nixon to create the first large scale air marshal program which was jointly administered by the FAA and the Department of Treasury, U. S. Customs Service.

Of all us who served are proud of our service and look back fondly on our friends and experiences. The program is in good hands in TSA and we can only hope that it will continue to exist in the future. We all wish to express our gratitude to the TSA for inviting all of the former sky marshals to participate in the 50th Anniversary and to meet those who are carrying on the tradition of "flying pigs."

Contents

Introduction

LEGENDS OF THE FLYING PIGS: MEMOIRS OF A FEDERAL SKY MARSHAL is a true story of the first Federal sky marshals or Customs Security Officers who flew the skies in the early 1970s to protect U.S. commercial airlines from hijacking. It is told through the eyes of the author who was one of the first of those trained by the Federal government in a crash program instituted by President Nixon after American aircraft were hijacked by Palestinian terrorists in September 1970 and flown to the Middle East and destroyed.

The tragic events of September 11, 2001 have brought about a revival of the air marshal program j under the Transportation Security Administration. If the original program had been maintained over the years, perhaps the horrific loss of life in New York, Washington and in the fields of Pennsylvania could have been prevented. Tragically, the first program lasted only about three years before the politicians and the airlines decided that it was more cost effective to rely upon technology and low paid private screeners. This book offers the lessons of the past to prevent the same mistakes in the future.

The book gives the details on the selection, training and operational techniques of the first U. S. Sky Marshals. It is both a serious and humorous story of young men and young women trained for six weeks, given weapons and put on aircraft to fly to every I location in the world. The author has collected the most interesting stories of his colleagues in the program and they are a mixture of sex, hours of boredom, hilarious mishaps in exotic spots around the world, and moments of pure terror when a hijacking seems to be unfolding.

This is a book appropriate at this time when everyone is concerned with air security and a new program is being implements to guarantee the safety of air passengers. The original sky marshals or "Flying Pigs" as they called themselves have a story to tell and some lessons to pass on to the next generation.

Chapter 1

AN EARLIER SEPTEMBER TRAGEDY

THE HORRIFIC EVENTS of September 11, 2001 were forever seated into the minds of Americans as we watched unbelievingly as the planes hit the Twin in New York, the Pentagon in Washington and another crashed into the field in Pennsylvania.

The immediate question, after the initial shock had ebbed, was how could something this terrible happen. How were the terrorists able to board four aircraft with box cutters and take over command of the planes? We believed that we had one of the best air security systems in the world with sophisticated X-ray equipment, magnetometers, and ion scan devices to test for explosive vapors and hand search of baggage.

Many will not remember another September, 31 years ago when another myth of air security was exposed as a fraud. Four aircraft including a Pan Am 747 and a TWA 707 were simultaneously hijacked and flown to a remote airfield in Jordan and Cairo. A fifth hijacking of an El Al flight was thwarted only by the bravery and diligence of Israeli sky marshals on board and the flight crew. The planes were blown up and the one hijacker, Leila Khaled, who was captured on the El Al flight after her partner Patrick Arguello, was killed by an Israeli sky marshal was released in return for the passengers on the four hijacked planes.

The public outrage and fear over these incidents forced governments around the world to take immediate action to restore confidence into the air transportation system. Before these events, hijacking of aircraft to Cuba was more of a nuisance than a serious problem. The planes were always returned, no passengers were harmed and the hijacker was Fidel's problem not ours. However the incidents in the desert on September 6 and 7 ended the notion that air piracy was a benign problem. Prior to these events, the only real precaution that was taken by the airlines was profiling of passengers based upon indicators such as paying cash, buying a one-way ticket, national origin of the passengers, lack of a legitimate reason for flying, etc.

However, in dealing with dedicated terrorists rather than amateurs, profiling was not always successful since the terrorist were aware of the profile carefully crafted their flight plans not to invite a more intensive examination.

The response in 1970 was similar in many aspects instill to the present response in so far as air security was concerned. President Nixon ordered the immediate deployment of sky marshal using Special Agents from which the various law enforcement agencies and military investigators. New laws passed and a new position makes was established in the Department of Transportation, Director of Civil Aviation Security. The President and the Secretary of Transportation named a noted military action. hero, General Benjamin O. Davis, Jr., to the post. General Davis, a pathfinder for Blacks in the military and a member and commander of the famous "Tuskegee Airmen", was given new authority to set security screening standards and to recruit a specially security trained air marshal force of over 2000 individuals.

General Davis and the Nixon administration put together a comprehensive Program consisting of placing armed Sky Marshals on most U.S. flag carriers. actual search of hand baggage by Federal officers to supplement the profile screening, international cooperation bilaterally and through the International Civil Aviation Organization and new technology such as magnotometers and baggage x-ray. as However, as in the case of many other law enforcement programs, once the immediate threat had faded, the politicians and the airlines convinced themselves that the program was too expensive and that they could rely on technology alone to do the job.

The initial air marshal program lasted only until 1973. A small number of air Marshals under the FAA was established in the 1980's to respond to immediate threats but this was mainly for cosmetic purposes to instill some doubt in the minds of those who might consider hijacking.

The FAA is an agency that is easy to criticize and which has been the target of both internal and external critics for years. Its close relationship with the airlines makes the Agency extremely reluctant to take any actions that the airlines oppose unless there is an over-whelming cry from the public or Congress to take action. It is often said that only the loss of human life can compel the FAA to take any action.

Those of us in the Customs Service have experienced the FAA's philosophy many times. In the 1980s, the Customs Service introduced an airport security program that required background checks and special holographic seals for airport personnel entering the Customs international inspection area.

I working in Tampa at the time with responsibility for airports in Tampa, Jacksonville and Orlando. As we began to process the airline and airport personell required to enter the Customs area, we were appalled at the results we were getting. We found out that many wanted felons even a murderer or two were working for the airlines and airports. The airlines and airports were doing only the most cursory background name checks and were not fingerprinting key employees to verify their true identities. The airlines and airports quickly complained that Customs was impinging upon their opera-tion and the FAA and DOT quickly complained to the Department of Treasury and the administration that Customs was usurping their authority and that the FAA would develop its own program. Recent events and disclosures on the lack of security at airports show the type of program they instituted.

In the case of the original air marshal program, the lack of any air piracy incidents after the 1970 tragedy in the deserts of the Mid-dle East gradually eroded the support for the program. Many of us in the Sky Marshal program felt the antipathy of the airlines towards any extra security measures and us. The airlines wish to make profits and anything that reduces the bottom line is viewed as a cost to be reduced or eliminated.

The air marshal program required the airlines to give up valuable passenger revenue on flights. It also had the potential of delaying flights due to pre-departure inspections of suspect passengers. The airlines were never convinced that the best solution was a confrontation in the air between armed hijackers and sky marshals. It was better to fly to whatever destination that the hijacker wished and then to negotiate the release of the airline, crew and passengers.

The parallels between 2001 and 1970 are striking but with obvious differences. The possibilities of using the hijacked aircraft as deadly suicide weapons raised the stakes for all concerned and rules out negotiations with the hijackers.

As General Davis pointed out in his autobiography, "Since the beginning of aviation in the United States, the federal government had not involved itself in airport security matters, leaving these problems to airport operators, airlines, and local authorities. I came to believe that the current situation demanded leadership and assistance by the federal government to ensure the safety of U. S. national and international air commerce." How prophetic those words sound today as once again national leaders echo the refrain that the federal government must be directly involved in air security. It is too large and expensive of a problem to be resolved by private or local entities.

If we had really learned and appreciated the lessons taught in 1970, we might have avoided the tragedy of September 11, 2001.

The only country and airline which has consistently and comprehensively dealt with air security are Israel and its national airline El Al. Knowing that it would always be a prime target of terrorists and surrounded by unfriendly Arab states, Israel has embraced a comprehensive approach to air security. It has used undercover air security officers on its airlines even prior to the 1970 incidents and as we will see they helped to thwart the attempted skyjacking of an El Al flight on September 6, 1970. In addition, they employ well-trained and experience security personnel on the ground to interview each passenger rather than only those who fit a profile. All ground personnel who work for El Al around the world must pass a rigid background check and of course they utilize the latest detection equipment to detect weapons and explosives in luggage. Their record of success in preventing air piracy of the destruction of their aircraft is impeccable and a model of what can be done if the government fully supports the program.

Of course, there is only one national airline in Israel and its number of flights and aircraft are miniscule compared to those in the United States. Duplication of their program in all of our airports and airlines would be costly and time consuming, but there is doubt that the public would accept anything less than a full court press effort after September 11. The challenge will be to establish a program and then to hold to the course as the shock of September 11 gradually subsides. It will need to be a flexible program that constantly reassesses the risks on the basis of intelligence supplied by the intelligence and law enforcement communities.

The next attempt will probably not be teams of five and box cutters but something different based upon an analysis of weaknesses in our air security program uncovered by terrorists or other groups seeking to blackmail airlines or for other causes as yet unknown. Technology will never supply all the answers and dedicated professionals are needed on the ground to question passengers and to ensure the security of the airport environs. El Al employs law enforcement professionals to question all passengers and there are revealing indicators of deception if any individual is being evasive about the purpose of travel.

To emphasize the need for trained security officers t and crew on board airlines as the last line of defense, I refer to a recent article by Robert Pollock in "Flight Watch". Pollock interviewed Uri Bar-Lev, the pilot on the El Al flight that was the subject of an on-board hijack attempt on September 6, 1970. Even though El Al utilized the best possible security checks on the ground, two terrorists were able to get on board the aircraft with weapons and attempt to take control.

"Just before takeoff of his El Al 707 from Amsterdam to New York on September 6, 1970, says Capt. Bar-Lev, security personnel approached him with the names of four suspicious passengers: two men in first class carrying Honduran diplomatic passports with consecutive numbers, and a blond couple also with Honduran passports in economy. The captain ordered the two in first class removed from the plane, and the couple searched.

But the search wasn't thorough enough. As the plane approached its cruising altitude of 31,000 feet, the cabin crew rang to alert him of a hijacking in progress. A man was holding a gun to the head of one stewardess, and a woman had pulled grenades from her brassiere. One steward attacked the male hijacker, who shot him five times.

The terrorists were demanding that Capt Bar-Lev 19 open the cockpit door. because—according to International Air Transport Association rules—he was responsible for the welfare of the passengers. But Capt. Bar-Lev quickly decided that he would have no control over their destiny if he surrendered. "My reply was: Sit down, we are not going to be hijacked."."

Figuring that almost everyone but the hijackers would be strapped in, Capt Bar-Lev put the plane into a negative -G dive—a downward arc often used to a train astronauts to experience weightlessness. Sure enough, the hijackers were thrown from their feet, and li the two plainclothes El Al marshals on board pounced. The male hijacker was killed, and the woman knocked unconscious. After her blond wig was pulled back, they realized that she was the notorious Leila Khaled, who had hijacked a TWA plane to Damascus the previous year in an attempt to capture Yitzhak Rabin, Israell's Ambassador to Washington (he had changed flights.)"

Hopefully this scenario will not occur again, but it shows that only a comprehensive air security program with trained aircrew and sky marshals working together with ground security can provide for the highest degree of safety for the aircraft and passengers. The United States had embarked upon such a program in 1970 but did not take the steps necessary to make it a permanent feature of air transportation. We are beginning again with a federal program and hopefully the lessons have been learned.

This books is both a historical and personal account of the United States Sky Marshal program in the early 1970s. I was a small part of the program and I am relying upon what I experienced along with the comments and accounts of my fellow sky marshals. It is a serious subject but the telling includes many comic and silly occurrences that happen when quickly recruit, train and arm a group of young men and women who are seeking adventure and trying to find out a little about themselves and their careers.

I do not claim or guarantee that all the stories are accurate and completely factual. In over 30 years, stories become embellished and memories become a little less accurate.

Chapter 2
HOW I BECAME A SKY MARSHAL

I WAS BORN in Roanoke, Virginia, a sleepy and ver.: conventional small southern city in 1947. I was the eldest of five children and my father was a newspaper editor for the afternoon paper. I guess I developed an addiction for newspapers and reading from him. My childhood was typical for the time and place, a lot of sports and hunting and fishing with my father and grandfather. However, I was a bit of a rebel and managed to get myself suspended from high school for the a few days in my senior year along with a few other in student leaders for skipping school to take part in the annual frolic of college girls at Hollins College col commonly called Tinker Days in which they climb the mountain directly behind the college. Needless to say we all got a stern lectures from the principal, parents, and teacher on the need to be responsible leaders and examples for our classmates.

One item of possible significance for my future ap employment was writing a novel for English class our about a secret agent named Jefferson Scott and his adventures in many exotic locations throughout the world. My good friend Mac Harris and I were avid and readers of Ian Fleming and the many adventures of James Bond. We longed for a life of adventure with guns and fast women in dangerous places. Perhaps it was just a reaction to life in a small city and our desires to travel.

It was also in high school that I met the girl who would eventually become my partner for life, Louise Fitzhugh. We were good friends even before we started dating and it would take me a number of years to finally realize that she was the ideal partner for me in life.

I resisted marriage for many years but time and Louise's patience convinced me that marriage to her was the right thing for me.

I entered the University of Virginia in 1965 and declared foreign affairs as my major.

I was always interested in other countries and other peoples in the world. I began to dream of a career in the Foreign Service and some other job that would involve travel to locations that I could barely locate on the globe. This was a time of great change in our college campuses as the Vietnam War was beginning to become more than just a faraway place. We had all registered for the draft but never gave it a second thought until the number of guys drafted began to increase and our college deferment begin to take on more significance. Also marijuana and hash began to appear a campus parties along with booze. We all got our first introduction to these forbidden experiences.

In the summer of 1969 after graduation from the University of Virginia, one of my roommates, Keith, and I headed west to California in the new Mustang that his family given him as a graduation present. It was a last escape before facing the realities of jobs, the military or more school. We followed the northern route, stopping at Mount Rushmore, Yellowstone and the Badlands, camping out most the time. Keith had relatives in a little town called Marshing, Idaho and we spent a few days fishing and riding Horses out to the areas inhabited only by Basque sheepherders and their flocks. Once a small child wandered right away and all joined in a massive search until we found the young boy.

We had two friends from the UVA Law School who had a summer job and apartment in Santa Monica and we ended up sleeping on their floor and couches. It was a crazy place and time. We enjoyed the beach, Dodger games, trips to the bullfights in Tijuana ant California girls and parties. It was tempting to there forever and lose oneself in the sun and laid-back was lifestyle, but we reluctantly left after a month ant unit headed back east along Route 66. I got my firs grad speeding ticket ever in Kingman, Arizona.

Upon graduation in June 1969, I had applied for graduate school at George Washington University in Washington, DC under a program sponsored by the Scottish Rite under which two outstanding students from each State who planned on either teaching or government service as a career were given full scholarships. This would also continue my draft deferment and very few of my fellow college grads were eager to enter the military to be sent to the escalating conflict pond in the rice paddies of Vietnam and the daily body counts.

Again I majored in International Affairs with an case, emphasis on Western Europe. However, events around us were beginning to effect us in ways that we could not envision. In Washington in 1970, the major peace marches were occurring and in the violent confrontations between students and police in clouds of tear gas; we were forced to confront the realities of our future. Graduate deferments were being phased out and a lottery was being installed. Our local draft boards were notifying us that we might be called to duty in the immediate future with no easy way out. As my first year of graduate school year was coming to an end, the first draft lottery was being held and my birthday was one of the lower numbers. I needed to do something if I did not wish to go into the military as a draftee. Through several friends I heard that the Virginia National Guard unit in Manassas, Virginia was actively seeking new enlistees. It was an Infantry unit that could be called to active duty, but with the gradual pullout of U.S. personnel from Vietnam it was unlikely that the Guard would be called to active duty.

I quickly applied to the unit and after some paperwork was duly enrolled in the 3rd Battalion of the 1 16th Division of the Army National Guard. I was directed to report to Fort Polk, Louisiana in September 1970 for the mandatory Basic and Advanced Individual Training. The spring session of graduate school ended without any further incident and I was pondering what my future occupation might be after the military training. I had always envisioned some type of Foreign Service or teaching, but as is often the case, J really did not have any strong conviction for a specific course of action.

I went home to Roanoke for a few months before reporting for active duty training. My high school sweetheart, Louise, was getting tired of waiting for me to commit to marriage and was planning to move to Atlanta with a friend to begin her nursing career. With all of the uncertainly in my future, I was not sure if marriage was something that 1 could handle at the moment. I went to my monthly drills in Manassas, which was about a three-hour drive from Roanoke. As my reporting date to Fort Polk drew near, I watched in as the Palestinian terrorists hijacked four jets to Jordan and Cairo and blew them up after getting another hijacker captured on El Al Airlines released.

For anyone who has gone through military training an at Fort Polk, I do not have to go into any great detail for you to recall what a hot and miserable place it was. In the late Summer/early Fall, the temperature and the humidity was enough to make anyone yearn for the North Pole. In my training company, we were equally th divided among draftees, enlisted and national/guard of reserve. The dividing lines were very clear in most cases.

The high school, farm kids and inner city kids were be the draftees and enlisted while all the college graduates were National Guard or reserve. Surprisingly there was little rancor between the groups. We were all suffering equally under the at physical strains imposed by the Drill Instructors and the fact that some of us were going home and others directly to Vietnam was present but not discussed. Our Drill Instructor was a Black Sergeant from the South who had already served a tour in Vietnam and had the shrapnel wounds to prove it.

He was a tough but fair individual. We were n classified as 11 Bravo or infantry and learned to operate every small arm in the U.S. arsenal including the M-16, M-14, M-60, M72 and all types of explosives and grenades. The biggest fear was that an accident with grenades or live fire exercises could result in your being killed by a fellow recruit. It happened to one recruit while we were at Fort Polk and a grenade that had slipped from a trainee's hand killed him and an instructor who was trying to rescue him. As an avid hunter and shooter from my childhood, I relished learning about all the weapons and usually managed to qualify as a sharpshooter or expert on each. The 45 caliber automatic is a notorious inaccurate handgun, but I enjoyed knocking the targets down with it.

I will always remember the long forced marches in the sun and swamps. You had to be careful in the field of coral snakes and alligators. The escape and evasion course was particularly memorable. We were let loose in the dark and had to cross a lot of ground without being caught by the opposition force. They scared us with the treatment we would get if captured so I was super careful and managed to crawl and hide until the morning came and not get caught. I missed everyone at home a lot and particularly, Louise. More and more I came to realize that life could be short and nasty and it was foolish to delay marriage if someone really loved you.

The one good thing was my physical condition. I was a lean and hard 160 pounds and felt that there was no physical challenge that I could not meet. After the first eight weeks of Basic Training, we infantry guys just moved to another section of the fort and began intensive training on infantry tactics and dealing with bobby traps and other risks we would face in Vietnam.

We begin to thank our lucky stars that we would not be boarding one of the transports to Vietnam after training and wishing the best of luck to the fellows with us who would be facing that faithful flight.

We did not get many weekend passes and the only place you could really go was either Lake Charles or Alexandria. These were small towns near the fort where unscrupulous individuals specialized in taking your money quickly through numerous bars, prostitutes, and motels with pools. The one time I went with some guys we just drank ourselves into oblivion and then swam and slept.

December arrived and we had our final graduation ceremonies and were given our plane trip back home. I had called Louine and arranged to go back through Atlanta to meet her and to go back home together. It was a wonderful time in Atlanta and then when I arrived home, my family had put up a big banner welcoming me home and the homecoming was wonderful and touching, One of the benefits of a large and close family is the feeling of warmth and security when one returns after a long absence.

Shortly after arriving home, I had given Louise a ring and had decided that we would get married soon after I found a permanent job. I sent my application into the Federal Government and also was sending applications to Junior Colleges to try to obtain a teaching position. To facilitate my job search, I arranged to move to Hillcrest Heights, Maryland to stay with my aunt while searching for a position. Job opportunities in Roanoke were limited or non-existent and I wanted to live in a large city.

In January, I received a letter offering me a position as a Customs Security Officer if I passed an initial interview and background check. I was directed to report to the Office of the Special Agent in Charge for Customs in Baltimore for the interview. The only questions that I dreaded were those dealing with prior drug use. As in the case of most college students in the 60s and 70s. I had tried marijuana and hashish at school.

It was a pleasant experience but one that I didn't need every week and I really preferred my bourbon or scotch rather than the smoking. I figured that they would find out if I lied so when the Customs investigator asked about prior drug use I acknowledged that I had tried it in college but not since then, which was basically true although there may have been one or two incidents after college.

It must have been the right answer since I was formally selected for GS-7 Custom Security Officer position and was given a reporting date for Treasury Air Security Officer School in January.

Chapter 3
TASOS (TREASURY AIR SECURITY OFFICER SCHOOL)

APART NOTIFICATION OF my selection as a Customs Security Officer/ Federal Sky Marshall, I was directed to report to Fort Belvoir, Virginia, An army base located on Route 1 approximately 25 miles from Washington DC. Fort Belvoir is the home of the Army Engineers. It is an older base with a typical brown wooden barracks that everyone has seen in old fluid WW II movies. It was a short drive for me from where I was living in Hillcrest Heights MD and we were directed to arrive on a Sunday to begin our training on Monday morning.

When I arrived at the base, we had to go through the military sentries at the gate and aner getting lost once or twice, I finally located the Treasury Air Security Office School orientation building. The official on duty verified my credentials and gave me thick packet of forms and material and assigned me to a room at the nearby barracks.

Since I had just concluded five months of active duty at Fort Polk, the surroundings were not unfamiliar to me. For those of you with a military background, it was equivalent to bachelor's officer quarters. The barracks was divided into small rooms each with two single beds with a dresser and chair. My roommate had already arrived and quickly introduced himself as Pete Douglas (name slightly changed to protect the innocent). Peter was character that I will never forget and I do not think that I have ever met anyone quite like him since.

He was a retired gunnery sergeant from the United State Marine Corps. As I was to learn in the days to follow, the Sky Marshal program was a coat of many colors. Those selected for the program ranged from the recent college graduates to retired military to furloughed airline personnel. As in the case of many crash government programs, there was no time or a carefully conceived recruitment plan for these new exotic federal employers who would fly throughout the world on U. S. air carriers. Anyone who was interested who did not have a criminal record and was physically capable of using weapons and subduing potential hijackers was deemed acceptable. There was little if any consideration of mental fitness and the type of individual who was best qualified to make a life or death decision that could affect the lives of 400 crew and passengers on a 747. The need for a more thorough psychological screening would become more obvious in the future as the new CSOs began flying and the incident reports began to flow in for disciplinary actions.

Back to Pete. I had met Marines previously and always thought that they were squared away type of guys. A little too straight with all the Semper Fi and Gung Ho attitudes perhaps, but people you could count on. With Pete, I saw a side of the Marines that I had never seen before. Pete had served the Corps around the world from the Philippines to Panama to Europe to places no one could even find on the map.

In each location he had served he seemed to have an unbelievable experience with brothels, prostitutes booze and brawls. From that first night that I listened enthralled as he described his encounters with wild hookers doing things on bar tables that I would have to see to believe, Pete opened my somewhat protected eyes to things that I had only heard occurred in XXX movies. I soon was to meet other marines in TASOS; all seemed to know or have heard of one another and had similar stories or could vouch for what the others were saying.

Pete was small in statue with curly brown hair, which was getting a little scarce on top. What he lacked in size, he made up for in toughness. He was the type of guy that you wanted to have by your side in any kind of fight. Pete never confirmed his age but it must have been about 40. He took me under his wing as a nice young fellow who had not seen much of the real world and needed a guide to show him how things worked and how to get into and get out of trouble.

The first day of TASOS was an introduction to the six-week program designed to turn us into dedicated agents of the air primed to detect and prevent any hijacking of U.S aircraft. Our instructors were a mix of Federal law enforcement personnel including Special Agents from Customs, ATF and the Secret Service, the uniformed White House Police who were our primary firearm instructors and various other experts from the FAA and the airlines.

It was clear from the beginning that the primary emphasis would be on the use of weapons inside the aircraft, hand-to-hand combat, and decision-making. There would be classroom instruction on Federal laws and regulations involving hijacking and arrests and on the layout and characteristics of various aircraft.

The daily schedule called for breakfast at 7-8 am followed by physical fitness and class, a break for lunch and then afternoon sessions until about 5pm. All food was served in a special mess hall that had been set up for us.

The most difficult part of the course for me was mastering the Smith and Wesson Model 16 .38 special revolver. I had fired guns and rifles all my life and considered myself a pretty good shot. I had also qualified with the .45 caliber automatic in the military training at Fort Polk. However the first part of the weapons qualification course required us to score a passing grade standing on a bull eye target from about 30 feet. The target was quite small and you had a limited amount of time to shoot the twelve qualifying rounds, which required one reload of the six shot Model 16 revolver with the six inch barrel. I was having a difficult time gently squeezing the trigger rather than jerking the shots too quickly.

Too many of my rounds were on the edge of the bull eye in a non-scoring position.

You had to pass the stationary bulls eye course before proceeding to the other firearms course, which involved silhouettes and a mock up of the interior of the aircraft.

The White House Police were good instructors and worked with me to improve my score.

I was getting more and more nervous as my classmates met the passing score and went on to more advanced shooting courses. My good friend, Pete, came to my rescue. Your partner did the scoring of the target for you as it was retrieved on a pulley from down the range. Pete simply used a bullet to put additional holes in the center of the target to give me the extra points I needed to qualify. What a relief to pass!!!

The hand-to-hand combat was also interesting. We learned all types of moves to disarm and incapacitate a suspected hijacker who had a gun, knife or other weapon. We were trained on how to put the handcuffs on a subdued hijacker and were also in the use of a black-jack to knock someone senseless or to break their hands. The black jack that we used and, which would be issued to us upon graduation along with her other equipment, was a lead ingot on a spring encased in leather. The spring effect gave it devastating striking power.

Our hand-to-hand combat was even more interesting due to the presence of the first female CSOs who were in her class. The women felt that they had to prove themselves the equal or better of any man and you dreaded having a women partner in the class since she would try to break your arm to get you to submit. However, I should point out that the female CSOs did extremely well in the program and many of them later moved up to high positions in the Customs Service and one, Bonnie Tischler, became an Assistant Commissioner.

It was made clear to us in the classroom sessions that as customs officers along with Deputy US Marshals we would have wide authority to search individuals we suspected of carrying weapons and contraband and to detain and arrest them under many different statutes.

As the days and weeks went by, we settled into the routine and got to know everyone in our class. I met four guys who would eventually become my roommates in New York and others who would show up later in my Customs career. On the weekends we went to the Officer Club at Fort Belvoir for drinks and I remember one wild night in downtown DC with Pete s and his marine buddies-a night that ended up at a house trailer near Quantico with several female Marines. I don't remember how or when we got back to Fort Belvoir that night.

The shooting became more and more interesting. The instructor explained that our Super Vel .38 caliber ammunition had some unique characteristics. It functioned like a dum-dum bullet and caused massive damage inside the body and did not come out the other side of the victim to cause damage to the plane. They showed us a movie clip in which the bullet hit a mass of meat blowing out the back side but with little force left in the round to penetrate the wall of an aircraft. Very impressive and a little scary!

The most realistic training was a firing range in which seats were set up as in the interior of an aircraft. Human silhouettes were used to act as simulated passengers. In the front of the aircraft mock up there was a hijacker silhouette. The drill was to hit the bad guy without hitting any passengers. You did not receive a passing score if you killed the passengers. To make it even more challenging, the lighting was dimmed and we had to shoot with both the left and right hand. Surprisingly, I did very well in this test.

We had numerous sessions of role-playing in which the instructors or other students pretended to be skyjackers grabbing passengers or aircrew personnel. We had to make quick decisions on when and what to do. We were continually warned not to reveal ourselves too soon since there could be more than 1 skyjacker on board. This was made more vivid in our minds by the story of the aborted attack on the El Al Flight where the two Palestinian hijackers. What we did not receive was any detailed psychological profiles on the motivations of hijackers. Some of us with educational backgrounds in international affairs understood the long standing struggle between the Arabs and the Jews. The religious fervor of those who deem themselves as oppressed and justified any actions against Israel and her Western supporters was never really laid out for us. It was just bad guys against us good guys and we were supposed to come out on top.

In retrospect, the training we received was excellent on the fundamentals of the criminal code and the use of weapons and hand to hand combat. It was it sorely lacking in giving us a profile or any indicators of individuals who might be preparing to skyjack an aircraft or take some other action which might resull in loss of life or control of the aircraft. Based upon the previous incidents and intelligence being gathered by other government agencies those in charge of the sky marshal program should have been able to give us a better picture of who might be involved in future actions against U.S. aircraft and the weapons and tactics that they might be using to gain control of the aircraft.

This may have been due to the traditional lack of cooperation and coordination between the FBI and the CIA and the belief of law enforcement professionals in the Department of Justice that any law enforcement officer associated with both Treasury and the FAA was someone who could not be trusted with sensitive information and was only a step above state and local cops or contractors. There is a strict hierarchy among law enforcement professionals and anyone below the rank of Special Agent or Criminal Investigator was considered a uniformed peon who could only be trusted to carry out the simplest functions.

As a result, none of us in my TASOS class knew anymore of the threat we were facing that the average citizen reading the newspapers and news magazines.

We were not given any information on terrorist networks and threat analyses of particular countries or airports. We were told that the threat was f rom those in the Middle East and those seeking to escape to Cuba. Any additional details were left to our own imagination and therefore many of us begin to distrust anyone of potential Arabic or Cuban heritage. It led to many mistakes and problems later on.

In our late night bull sessions back in the barracks, several expressed the opinion that it was better to be judged by 12 rather than be carried by 6.

In other words, it was better to shoot an innocent person rather than to be killed yourself through hesitating to act in a suspicious circumstance. We felt that we were basically alone with our partners in the air and that in the absence of information, we were going to take action in any circumstance which might lead to hijacking or shoot out.

All of the prospective Sky Marshals in Class 5 were beginning to know each other by now. As a graduation approached we began to speculate on our future assignments. Most of us wanted to fly on TWA or Pan American to go to foreign destinations. Each week however a few students dropped out or were called to the office and were removed from the program due to information found in their background checks. None of us from the civilian side were aware that we were given just an initial clearance to enter the program on the basis of a national agency check using our fingerprints. A more detailed full-field investigation was launched using investigators to verify our character and our answers to various questions by interviewing people who knew or worked with us. There was a feeling of doubt each time received a call or note fearing that someone from our past might say that you were Communists or serial killers.

I had mentioned some casual drug use in college to my initial interviewer and I was a little afraid that my definition of casual use might differ from that of the U. S. government.

Along with Pete and his marine buddies, I became good friends with a group of young guys my own age who were just out of college and looking for excitement and travel.

Their names were Phil, Will, and John (again alias to protect them). They all were from Boston or New England and we shared many good bull sessions on college, girls, sports and the foreign destinations that we hoped to see.

Graduation Day finally arrived and we lucky graduates were busted into Washington for graduation ceremonies. If my memory is correct the Assistant Secretary of the Treasury for Enforcement, Eugene Rossides, was present and someone from FAA. Sure if it was General Davis the people were all too excited to care. We received our credentials and government issue equipment, which were quite impressive. They included the following:

- one Model 16 Smith and Wesson Revolver
- one black jack
- one pair of handcuffs
- badge #1674 and credentials as a Customs Security Officer
- credentials as a deputy U. S. Marshal

- two passports (one official and one tourist)

We also received our assignments and to my excitement, I was directed to report to John F. Kennedy Airport in New York and to begin as a Sky Marshal on Pan American World Airlines prayers had been answered; I was going to see the world at government expense.

Chapter 4
NEY YORK, NEW YORK

WE WERE GIVEN a week or so off after graduation to put our affairs in order and were given tickets and told to check in at a motel in Queens not far from JFK. I had a chance to go to Roanoke to see Louise and we made plans for a wedding in July. I finally made a commitment to tie the knot although I really did not know what to expect in my life over the next four months.

Fortunately, several of my good friends from TASOS Class 5 also were also assigned to New York. Pete was not and we had to say goodbye. I told him how much I appreciated his support and guidance through the program that I would try to avoid some of the red light districts and bars around the world that the Marine Corps had made famous (or infamous).

We arrived in New York on a Saturday night and took cabs to the motel in Queens. Some of the reason graduates took their cars and for some it was a rude awakening to the big city. Tom, a furloughed American Airlines pilot drove his price BMW 2000 up to the motel lodge and lo and behold it was stolen on the second night in New York. Most embarrassing was the fact that his pistol was locked in the trunk of the car. The car and the weapon were eventually recovered but it was an early lesson to all of us that we had to be a little more careful.

The Customs Security Office Headquarters at JFK was in a nondescript office in Far Rockaway near the Beach. I was not sure why they picked such an isolated location, perhaps the rent was cheap where they wanted to have a place off the airport that would not draw any undue attention. The staff that worked in the office and did the scheduling and assignments would be the object of much derision and bad feelings. Those of us who were flying always felt that the schedulers took care of their buddies and gave the rest of us the most undesirable assignments. I guess it is the same feeling that the grunts in the field have forced those in cushy rear echelon posts.

After checking in at the CSO office we were taken to the UTV of JFK the home of Pan Am. In the 70s Pan Am was the premier U. S. International Air Carrier. It proudly traced its history back to the days of Lindberg in the famous Pan Am Clipper flying boats that crossed the Pacific. Although other U. S. carriers such as TWA and Northwest also had international flights Pan Am flew only international flights and its blue emblem was known and respected worldwide.

The flight crews were also usually quite senior aner coming over to work for Pan Am from other airlines. There was a certain haughtiness in their attitude towards other airline personnel, and, as we were to find out, the interlopers with guns who were going to fly in their planes and perhaps cause them problems.

Three of the guys from my class in TASOS were assigned to JFK with me although not to Pan Am. They were Walter, Bill and Chip. All from New England with broad accents and a willingness to have a little fun. we decided to go in together to find an apartment near JFK and went through an apartment rental service to find one. It was a second floor two-bedroom unit near 125th and Lefferts Boulevard in Queens near the bus line to JFK.

It was a neighborhood with some fine local bars and close to a watering hole named the "Salty Dog", which was a popular gathering spot for off-duty flight crews and JFK personnel. We did not spend very h much money on furniture.

The apartment had two beds and a couch along with a table and chairs. The neighborhood was also well known for the killing of Kitty Genovese who was brutally killed outside of an apartment building while d others heard her screams but did not intervene.

New York bars were a pleasant surprise after the ones we patronized in other cities. Once you had established yourself as part of the regular cliental, you could expect to have the bartender give you a drink on the house after you had been drinking for a while.

We would become familiar with a number of the crews and many had great stories of places around the world they had visited and the most fun things to do and purchases to make.

We did not expect the four of us to be at home at the same time because of our flight schedules. If all four happened to be there at the same time, someone would sleep on the couch or we would take the mattress off of one of the beds and put it on the floor so that everyone could have someplace to sleep. We decorated the apartment in full male law enforcement style, complete with pin ups.

We tacked up targets full of bullet holes, along with sports memorabilia (all of the other guys were diehard Red Sox fans). We put our guns, shoulder holsters, blackjacks, handcuffs and spare rounds on tables, chairs and on hooks. If one came into the room unaware of the occupants, it looked like a pad for the Mafia.

If one the guys was entertaining a lady, we had a "do not disturb" sign that we had filched from some hotel and it was a cardinal rule not to enter the room without checking for the sign or listening for conversation.

At JFK, we got an intensive orientation on our duties from the various airlines to which we were assigned. In addition, the Customs Special Agents and other law enforcement officers who had been flying since September 1970 while we were being trained gave us some practical hints on how to get the job done.

We were shown the various aircraft flown by Pan Am in great detail. The areas that contained the aircraft's hydraulics were pointed out and we were warned never to shoot a round in those areas or everyone would go down in flames. We were shown ways in which we could enter the cockpit in the 747 without going through the main cockpit door. There is—or was—a small door off the cocktail lounge near the restroom that could be used if we needed to use it to enter the cockpit unnoticed. On the DC-10s and L10-11s, there were multiple elevators that were used by the flight crew in cooking meals and these could be hiding places for hijackers or for us if necessary.

The preferred Sky Marshal coverage of an aircraft was two marshals on a 707 or any smaller aircraft with three on a wide body.

One CSO would be in first and the other in economy on a smaller jet and one in in first class and two in economy in a wide body. We would alternate first class on each leg of the flight.

In those days, first class on a Pan Am flight was really an experience to be savored. Only the very rich and famous could afford such travel and the airline went all out to give the first class passengers a memorable trip with all the accouterments of a five-star restaurant. Champagne and caviar served from the beginning and the foods was cooked on the aircraft and served on the best linen and china. We eagerly awaited our turn to ride up front and pretend that we really belonged with the moneyed elite who could in afford such extravagance.

In our discussions with the airline security personnel and previous Sky Marshals, it was pointed out that we needed to be able to convince the passengers and potential hijackers of our two identities. No one except the aircrew was supposed to know who we were and our safety and the safety of the plane depended on us being anonymous. To fool those pr around us who might wish to play "guess the Sky Marshal", we were asked to develop believable cover stories to set up an identity that would explain who we bo were and why we were flying. Most of us developed a persona that was not too complex so that we would not get caught up in our own fabrications and end up giving ourselves away with too much detail. Many of us just told the curious or that were off duty airline personnel taking a free holiday on the airline, one of the perks of being employees. Since we all were issued airline ID cards in order to get into the restricted areas of JFK and to identify ourselves to other airline personnel, this was easy to do. However some of us were unfulfilled thespians and developed storylines which were designed for Academy Awards. One CSO, who will remain nameless, took the grand prize. He has over 20 different business cards printed with his alter ego's and interchanged them around the world. On one flight he was a salesman of cameras, on another a tour operator, and another a movie talent scout. We all thought he was a little wacky but he enjoyed the roleplaying and I don't think that he was ever uncovered in one of his false identities.

We were told that we would alternate between flying status and ground duty.

In ground duty we would work with Customs Inspectors to search the hand baggage of departing passengers. The magnetometers were just being deployed in airports and the President and the FAA were using hand baggage search along with the profiles to try to detect high-risk persons before they boarded the aircraft. The plan was for us to fly for two month and then do a month of ground duty during preboarding baggage inspection under the guidance of an experienced Customs Inspector. As we were to find out, the scheduling of the ground inspection duties was not quite perfected and we were to enjoy some nice free time until the schedulers were able to get organized.

All of us took advantage of the free time to update our wardrobes with some nice suits and topcoats purchased in the small shops in the garment district New York. The carrying of weapons, handcuffs, black. jacks and other enforcement equipment called loose fitting garments that would not show any distinct shapes.

We gained an appreciation of the nightlife in York; learning of the after-hours clubs that opened after the bars shut down. I gained my life long love Irish Stout in the Irish pubs of the city.

My first flight on Pan Am was scheduled. I was to commence my two-month flight time with a around flight to Frankfurt which was a key European hub for Pan Am and the gateway to flights to the East and Asia. Before the day arrived—it was March 17 in New York—and I was introduced to St. Patrickck's Day in the big city. We watched the parade and visited half the bars in New York before collapsing into our beds in the wee hours of the morning. What a life!

Chapter 5
FIRST FLIGHTS

My name showed up on the schedule posted in the C SO office and I was ready to start my flying career.

I was booked for two months of flight duty then to report for a month of ground duty at Dulles International Airport. My initial flight was a turn around Pan Am flight to Frankfurt. I would arrive in the morning and then fly back to JFK the next afternoon. It was a 707 flight and I had one of the marines that I had met in Fort Belvoir as my partner.

The routine for a flight was exciting at first, but later would become a pro forma routine. We would report to the UTB about two hours before the flight and attend the pre-flight briefing with the crew. The crew would get a chance to meet us and get the seat assignments that we would be using during the flights. We gave a little speech on our duties, which were to protect them and the passengers from any threat on board. We would order verbally an alcoholic drink such as a Bloody Mary or Screwdriver, but they would prepare it without alcohol. If they noticed any suspicious passengers or activities, they could pass us a note on the cocktail napkins. We would be staying at the same hotel as the aircrew upon our arrival in Frankfurt, but in most cases, we would ride to the hotel separately since we had to deposit our weapons in a safe and secure area of the airport before departing. Most of the flight crew seemed to welcome or accept our presence although it was clear that the senior pilots had reservations about us being on board. It would take a while for us to understand the dynamics and status of the flight crews.

Many of the senior pilots or co-pilots had relationships with some of the stewardesses. We flew together and partly together upon their arrival at the destination city. The flight attendants who were not paired off with someone usually hung out together and would sometimes invite us to go places with them. We all knew the best restaurants and shopping areas in each foreign destination and you could never go wrong by listening to their advice.

After the briefing, we went upstairs to the retain passenger terminal and began to merge with the other passengers awaiting the flight. We tried to identify anyone who was suspicious in dress, conversation or activity. At the time of boarding, the CSOs, airline hotel personnel or others doing the pre-departure search hotels knew who we were by a mark on our tickets. We were large allowed to pass through without any personal search was which would have quickly revealed the Smith and Wesson in a shoulder holster on my left side, the desti blackjack in my coat pocket and the handcuffs in my briefcase.

The first flight was exhilarating! I was on my way and to see the world. I was in first class on the way over get u and the food and service was exceptional. As plane know flew on into the darkness towards Europe, the other the passengers dozed or read, but I was nervously trying gettin to identify anyone who might pose a threat. I opened a book but only read a few paragraphs. Later as things stayin became more routine, I would have to fight off sleep and drink many cups of coffee to stay awake. Sleeping on a flight was a serious viola-tion that could cost us our jobs and some crew members were eager to report us if we nodded off.

As the sun arose in the East, we touched down at Frankfurt Main Airport. After disembarking, we let the other passengers clear German immigration and customs before identifying ourselves to the German authorities. We were then directed to an office contain-ing a safe in which we would store our until departure. With few exceptions none of the foreign countries we visited would allow us to retain our firearms during our stay. We would be required to unload our weapons and store the bullets separately from the weapon.

My partner and I then took a taxi to a wonderful old hotel near the downtown central train station. The hotels used by Pan Am were topnotch. The beds were large and soft with down comforters and the furniture was beautiful heavy dark wood.

The biggest decision upon arrival at the hotel in the destination city was whether to take a nap immediately or keep going until the evening. The old German hotel had wonderfully soft and fluffy eider down comforters and once you sank down in them you did not wish to get up again. As all frequent international travelers know, the time change makes it difficult to sleep when the sun goes down in the destination. Your body is getting mixed communications and it wants to sleep during the day and stay up all night. If you are only staying a day, you do not have time to adjust to the different time. I tried it various ways and never managed to find a permanent solution. Sometimes I took a few hours nap on arrival and then found it hard to go out for the evening and get back to sleep during the night. If my partner wanted to go out shopping or sightseeing upon arrival, I always try to go with him since it was an unwritten rule that you would always be there to support your partner in cases of trouble.

Frankfurt was the most Americanized city that routinely visited. Most of the inhabitants English as a result of the occupation after WWII had a warm regard for Americans due to our support of them through the Marshall Plan and the Berlin airlift. There was a small bar on the Kaiser Strauss Is there a street named Elsa's that became the unofficial watering for American in the world Sky Marshals. The owner, Elsa, was an engaging lady with many good stories from the war. She had married an American GI and was more than happy to serve us beer at a good price and tell us about the diversions in Frankfurt.

My ex-Marine partner was eager to get to a place called the Crazy Sex. It was housed in an old building in the red light district in which beautiful young German prostitutes would stand in the alcoves of the first floor and you would approach them for service and a quick visit to their rooms upstairs. They all had their health cards from the German authorities and their rooms were tastefully decorated. Usually they had an album of their most alluring photos, which the: showed you to get you started and a ready supply of condoms, which they demanded that you use. With some of my partners, this was always the first stop the early evening. I preferred a meal in the Saxon Hauss area of the city near the University in the wine bars. Frankfurt was not a particularly scenic city especially since they were installing a subway system and there was a lot of construction underway. We visited some of the churches and other points of interest, but usually it was drinking and eating. Supposedly we were not supposed to have any alcoholic beverages within 24 hours of flight but this was widely ignored by us as well as the flight crew. As long as you did not drink in the morning the flight, you could do anything you wished the night before.

We usually slept in late on the next day and headed for the airport at about 9 a.m. for a flight in the late morning or early afternoon. We would pick up our weapons in the German customs area and then go to the passenger gate.

Again the ticket agents would put an identifying mark on our tickets so that the ground searchers would pass us through with a minimum of questions.

The first flight ended uneventfully back at JFK and the next day we were in the air again on our next flight. We usually had a different partner or partners for each flight. Some you quickly became great friends with and others you hoped that you never see again. As the flights continued and the days passed, exhaustion and ennui became bigger problems. Pilots are restricted to about SO hours of flight time a month under FAA regulations. There were no such limitations for us and some of us began to fly over 120 hours a month. Trying to keep alert in such circumstances is very difficult. The initial excitement gives way to boredom as you spend long hours in the restricted cabin space and the constant change of time zones plays havoc with your sleep.

All of us initially scrutinized every passenger in great detail. We tried to read their minds and every action that they talked to find out if they posed a threat to us on the plane. Every action someone took appeared to us to be full of potential danger. If they got up suddenly to go to the john or to open their briefcase, we instantly tensed up to prepare for a sudden appearance of a gun or grenade. If two guys poked one another we immediately feared a conspriacy and a rush to the cockpit. These initial feelings of danger and threat diminished as we flew more miles and got acquainted with the odd things that people did on aircraft.

Some passengers especially in first class looked and behaved as you would expect. They were seasoned international travellers who dressed well and knew how to pass time through reading, playing cards, or sleeping. Their conversation was polite and they were obviously well educated and urbane.

However, in first class you also had those who were rich but who dressed and behaved a little differently. They tended to be loud and often drank too much and talked too loud. We soon learned that we had nothing to fear from these individuals who were often asleep after a few too many drinks and passes at the stewardesses.

In economy class, it was much more difficult to ascertain the background and motivations of the passengers. We tended to look more closely at the young males and females who were neither Western European or American. We began to focus on their movements and if they paid too much attention to the flight crew and those around them. In our minds. we identified those who to us presented the greatest risk and how we would intercept them if they made a move towards the flight crew or to the front of the aircraft. All of us had experiences in which we were sure that an individual was planning to do something but in almost all cases, it was our unfamiliarity with their culture that led us to read too much into small gestures. Close scrutiny of the persons around you on a plane is a habit which is difficult to unlearn. I and the other CSO's always find ourselves looking closely at the clothing of others to spot any budges and to be aware of any sudden movements. I have never been able to sleep on a plane since my days as a CSO and it makes for some long flights and a crash into the first bed at the airport of destination.

We also become familiar with the young lovers anxious to join the "Five Mile High Club" We could see the foreplay and kissing began and we watched closely to see how they would manage to have intercourse in a crowded 747 without drawing the attention of all the other passengers. Sometimes, they would go one by one to the lavatory and sneak into one together. Sometimes it was more brazen as they covered themselves with a blanket in the dark with the lady straddling the man and began to move in slow motion together. Strange things happen on aircraft late at night and sometimes it involved two of the flight crew who knew the better hiding places.

Children on aircraft were both a blessing and a curse. It was hard to believe that a young Middle Eastern couple with a child posed a serious threat to the aircraft. The use of children as a cover for terrorists was not even a real concern then. If a child was present, we automatically took them off of our mental list of potential bad guys. However, children on a long flight refused to sleep or seized crying wore a real problem. We couldn't put earplugs in our ears or move away from our assigned seat. If a child wished to cry all night on a flight, we would simply have to endure it and keep our attention on our duties.

Another problem that I quickly became aware of was lower track distress or the dreaded touristas. As we ate rich food on board the aircraft and the local specialties in each country we visited, our digestive systems began to rebel.

We spent a lot of time in the toilets on board the aircraft and quickly run to the nearest WC upon arrival. My worst case came on a flight to Rome. I was suffering from cramps and frequent runs to the toilet before we reached Rome. Upon checking in at the hotel in Rome, my partner beefed me to the head (We always share the room for cost efficiency). I had a desperate and undeniable need to take a crap. Looking around the room, the only thing I could find was a large wine goblet. I quickly grabbed it just as my sphincter muscles failed me and filled the goblet to overflowing. As my partner finished, I rushed into the toilet and finished the process. What a mess!

The same trip to Rome almost left me behind at Leonardo De Vinci International Airport, Prior to departure we were slumped into the gents in the departure lounge. I was still recovering from many toilet trips and was dozing o little. The flight began to board and I groggily headed for the aircraft door. As I walked inside, I checked my gun and passport and to my horror my passport case was missing, I quickly turned to the flight crew told them that I must go back into the terminal. They told me that there was no time but I rushed back anyway past the startled Italian security guards with their submachine guns to the lounge area. Sure enough, my passport case was there. I then ran to the aircraft door, which had just been closed and beat upon it until they opened and let me in. That was the closest I came to missing a flight. I was later to learn that a number of CSOs had missed flights and sometimes it took quite a time to get new tickets and get back to the U. S. In one incident, which quickly became a legend for the Sky Marshal program, a CSO missed a flight from Casablanca, Morocco and was not seen again for two weeks. His story was a nightmare of missing documents and government red tape in getting a new passport issued. We all believed that it was simply a case of getting a little extra R and R.

My first flight to Heathrow in London was also an eye opener. There was a little security room in which you were supposed to unload your weapon and then put the weapon and bullets separately into a safe. Early in the Sky Marshal program, an anxious CSO forgot to take his finger away from the trigger while unloading and scared everyone in the airport by shooting a hole in the wall into the next room. The British authorities with a typical example of British humor had posted a sign requesting that American Sky Marshals please aim at the floor when unloading their weapons. We never heard what happened to the unfortunate CSO responsible for the accidental discharge.

It was also during my first flight to London that we met some El Al and Aeroflot air security personnel. The El Al officers were true professionals with military and civilian training. They had Uzis as well ba as side arms. It was clear to them that their lives and the lives of other Israelis would be on the line and they would not hesitate to use all the force at their disposal be to prevent a hijacking. The Soviet guards looked like to military personnel. There was no undercover need for them. They sat in the front of the plane with their of weapons ready to shoot anyone who stood up without co permission.

As the first two months of flights continued, I flew to other exotic places and each held a new adventure. The flight to Beirut was an eye opener. In the 70s, Beirut was considered the Paris of the Middle East.

We stayed in the Phoenicia Intercontinental just up the hill from the Royal St. George yacht basin with all the glamorous watercraft of the rich and famous. When you arrive in the lavishly decorated hotel lobby, waiters with fezzes offered you sweet Turkish coffee from large decanters. The hotel bar was famous throughout the world. It was built below the swimming pool and you could watch the bathing beauties through a panorama glass window. In my first trip to the bar, I saw several familiar faces from the movies and television. Broderick Crawford, who played in "Highway 410", Was there holding court with a sweet young starlet and he was obviously feeling no pain and telling ribald stories.

The flight crew on that trip was extraordinarily friendly and took my partner and me to the gold and carpet markets in the bazaar. Determined salesmen surrounded un and they plied us with drinks and sweets. Every time we tried to leave, they pulled us back to offer a better deal. For a while, I was getting worried that we would not be able to leave until we bought something and what they were selling was beyond our meager means. We finally were allowed to leave after pleading poverty. One thing all of us purchased was a camel saddle chair. This was a device of wood and leather that you assemble to make a comfortable seat. They were very cheap and I think everyone who went to Beirut purchased one. 1 enjoyed mine for many years until the wood and leather finally expired.

Other flights followed, a flight to Paris and our first visit to the Left Bank, the Moulin Rouge and Place Pigalle. We went to the famous Crazy House Saloon and ogled the fabulous nude dancers. Also a trip to Cannes and the French Rivera. Most of our flights were either three days or five days to Europe. I only had one flight to South America, to Caracas, Venezuela.

After Europe, the contrast was dramatic. A flight into the airport near the ocean at sea level and then a limo ride up the mountain to Caracas. All along the road, we saw the shanties and shacks of the poor. What a difference in the city itself with modern hotels and sky scrappers.

On a flight to Brussels, I teamed up again with one of my old marine buddies from Fort Belvoir, Phil. He was an Afro-American who considered himself the world greatest lover. In every location that I flew with him, his one desire was to meet an eligible female in our city of destination and to score with her in one night. On this flight to Brussels, Phil met some nice young American schoolteachers from New York on a visit to Europe. Phil quickly arranged for us to meet with them after our flight at a cafe on the Grand Place. We had a nice beer with them and I was ready for dinner and an early sleep. For Phil, the night had just started. He woke me up at about 2 a.m. and with a big smile, indicated that his quest had been successful. I just smiled and went back to sleep.

Lisbon was another interesting location. We all took a bus down to the casino at Estoril and enjoyed losing our money at the tables and watching the high rollers at the Baccarat tables.

Then my name came up for the big one. Flight 1 to Bangkok and return.

This was Pan Am's around the globe flight. Flight 1 left from New York and Flight 2 from San Francisco. The eastbound and westbound met in Bangkok and the crews switched aircraft and returned to their departure point. It was a full 14-day circuit. The 747 first flew to Frankfurt and then to Istanbul or Beirut. Then eastwards to either New Delhi or Karachi and then finally to Bangkok. Many hours on the aircraft but you usually had a two-day layover in either Delhi or Karachi and then a three-day break in Bangkok. We all looked forward to these flights that took us to far away places with scenic sites to visit and different foods and activities to try. In Delhi for the first time, I will always remember arriving one night when some type of large flying bugs was infesting the airport. It was impossible not to stomp on them and they made a horrible sound as they popped under our feet. Everyone took the bus or plane to the Taj Mahal and explored the Red Fort and Gandhi's tomb. We enjoyed the trips to the markets and purchased leather goods and brass items. I still have a rabbit hat that I purchased that made me look like a mad Kamikaze pilot. The most difficult sight for us to deal with was the beggars. We realized that this is a profession in India but the horrible deformed men, women and kids made us easy targets for donations. At the Intercontinental Hotel, they served wonderful ice tea with mint and little pitchers of sugar water. It was great to relax around the pool and observe the different nationalities and cultures.

We soon learned of that infamous malady known as the "Delhi belly". It seemed as if the Indian cuisine with its exotic curries and spices had an unfortunate effect on the Western digestive system. We were told the woes of a previous Sky Marshal lay over in Delhi that became an extended stay. One of a team of three came down with the "Delhi belly" and spent over a week marooned in-country trying to recover enough to board a plane back to the States. He was treated by a number of local physicians but nothing seemed to work. He could not keep any food in his system and appeared to be shrinking before everyone's eyes. Each day that another team of Sky Marshals flew into Delhi, they would immediately check with the hotel to see if he was still in bed and alive. Finally after a week, he had recovered sufficiently to limp on board an East bound Pan Am flight. When he finally arrived back in New York, He kissed the tarmac and shortly after submitted his resignation. So much for the life of international travel and exotic meals.

In Karachi, we all soon learned about Captain

Charlie and his boat trips out to an island in the Arabian Gulf for a day of sailing, fishing, swimming had and eating. There also the camel rides on the beach.

However, Pakistan was a Moslem country with strict requirements on alcoholic beverages and other Western vices. We had to be pretty careful of where we went and what we did. There seemed to be daily riots of the students for various causes. No pork products so we had to be satisfied with beef and lamb.

The highlight of the trip was the three-day layover doll in Bangkok. We usually stayed at the Siam we Intercontinental or President Hotels. There were trips the on the canals, visits to the snake farms (l still have a photo of me with a 70-foot python draped around my and neck) and the wonderful bargains in clothing, opals, and jewelry. However, most of the guys wanted to our take advantage of the sex life in Bangkok. As a result of the R&R by US military personnel stationed in Vietnam, a thriving sex scene existed in Bangkok. Upon arrival at the hotel we were introduced to a guide who would stay with us for a day or two.

He first took us to a house in the city that had a one-way mirror through which one could view all the beautiful young Thai prostitutes lounging in the waiting area. All were very young and many spoke excellent English. After you made your selection, you were introduced and you and the girl took off for a night on the town at the best restaurants and dance spots. They accompanied you to your hotel room and gave you the pleasure of a back massage with their bare feet. After a night of pleasure, you had breakfast together and said goodbye. Not until later did you begin to question how old the girl really was and if she had been forced into a life of prostitution. I had several older partners who took the light in finding the youngest girls possible. It was a little too weird to see a graying American with someone young enough to be his daughter.

Another highlight of a trip to Bangkok was the shopping for jewelry and custom made clothing and a visit to the snake farm. The exchange rate of US dollars for Thai currency was very much in our favor. We were told of the best tailors and jewel merchants in the city and quickly went to their premises upon arrival. We would order customs made shirts and suits and often they were ready in 24 hours. We always looked good coming back from a trip to Bangkok in our new duds. Also you could buy beautiful opals and other precious stones and they craftsmen would set them into rings, earrings, necklaces and other types of jewelry. My wife treasures a pair of Australian fire opals earrings to this day and I was never able to find the equivalent in any US stores.

The visit to the snake farm was a "must do" for the first time visitor to Bangkok. We took a taxi a location on the outskirts of the city and were ushered into a fenced enclosure teaming with all types reptiles. The king cobras and spitting cobras were exciting creatures to see and the handlers put on a wonderful show. The test of manhood was to agree let them put a large python around your neck to take a souvenir photo. My time came for the test and the python they chose was about 12 feet long and weighed over 80 pounds. I could barely hold it by the head it wrapped itself around me.

They were used to being handled so that I was in any real danger, but the strength of the snake we unbelievable and it was all that I could do to keep head pointed away from my face. We celebrated feat with many bottles of good Thai beer that night.

My first two months of flight duty were coming to an end and I welcomed the break. I was so exhausted on a flight to London that I found myself dozing off in the upper cocktail lounge of a 747 and unfortunately the captain saw me before I could rouse myself and threatened to report me for sleeping on duty.

I tried to explain that I had flown too many hours and that I was doing all that I could to keep awake. I am not sure if he ever reported me but there were no consequences. During the two months of flying, the CSO office would try to schedule us for pre-departure inspection duties when we were on the ground in New York for more than two days, but usually they could not contact us and we were free to take off and enjoy ourselves. My month of ground duty would be at my home port of Dulles and I welcomed the chance to see Louise in my family.

Chapter 6
GROUND DUTY AND THE CUSTOMS SERVICE

I LEFT NEW York and returned to Dulles to perform my month of ground duty. Louise and I were also getting married and I had to catch up with my drills with the Virginia National Guard. Even though I was Fed flying on government duty and could not possibly bac attend the monthly weekend drills, I was still gigged for missing the drills, reduced in rank and counseled that I would be put on active duty if I continued to miss any future drills.

It was becoming evident that I needed to find another job that would allow me to meet my military as well as husbandly obligations. I could not do so by flying constantly for two months at a time. Being a Sky Marshal was definitely a job for young single men and women with no other commitments.

At Dulles, we were charged with doing all the pre-departure inspections of passengers and also helping in the international passenger arrival area as the uniformed armed enforcement officers to assist the Customs Inspectors. Our ground supervisors were old time Customs Patrol Officers who were basically guards on search teams at the seaports used to dealing with crewmembers smuggling drugs or alcohol. They were not too pleased to have to deal with a butch of wild and crazy Sky Marshals who definitely were not old school. One of our two supervisors at Dulles was pretty understanding and told us a lot about Customs and its day-to-day working.

The other was a real prick who delighted in writing us up for any minor violation of procedures. He never had flown and resented those of us who had.

For the first time, I learned a little more about the Agency that would become my career employer.

Customs wass a unique agency in the U. S. Government and is extremely proud of its mission and heritage. It prides itself on being the second oldest Federal agency with an unbroken history stretching back to 1789. At that time, it had over 300 ports of entry around the country and was organized into Districts and Regions. In the early days, a Customs officer position was viewed as quite a plum job and fit many famous persons such as Herman Melville served lite as Customs officers.

Customs duties were the prime source of government revenue until the income tax was introduced in the 20th century. Customs is one of the few agencies that actually collects more revenue than it spends.

As a Customs Security Officer I was working for the Customs Agency Service under the leadership of the Special Agent in Charge. This is now the Office of Investigations and the Customs Special Agents represent one of the three primary Customs occupations.

In the 1970s, there were relatively few Customs Special Agents who were plain clothes criminal investigators in the same classification series with Special Agents for the FBI, DEA, Secret Service, and ATF. In the 70's most of the Special Agents were Customs officers who had served in some other section of Customs before Special Agents. Their status was unique in Customs and they staffed our Attache offices. Later the increased drug led Customs to bring more Agents on board who came from Police narcotic squads who had little knownledge or appreciation of the commercial activities of Customs and they were solely interested in narcotics undercover activities or money laundering. Along with the Special Agents who were the elite in the enforcement side of Customs, there were uniformed Customs officers known as Customs Patrol Officers, Customs Port Investigators and of course, us, the Customs Security Officers.

The CPOS and CPIs were responsible for security at the docks and airports along with searching vessels and aircraft. On the land borders, they had a more extensive role in patrolling similar to the Border Patrol.

They also had small boats to complement the Coast Guard in maritime enforcement.

The Customs Patrol Officers were eventually abolished in the 1980s and the numbers of Special Agents was increased. Additional specialist positions such as Customs pilots and marine officers were added as the number of enforcement positions was expanded. As the Customs Security Officer program was being phased out in 1973, individuals who remained were converted into Customs Patrol Officers.

As I was to learn during my month of ground duty, the second primary occupation group of the Customs Service was the Customs Inspectors. They were the uniformed officers responsible for interviewing and searching arriving passengers and examining cargo entering the United States.

The Customs Inspectors a lucrative pay system known as the 1911 Law which for 1/2 day pay for each two hours worked tie normal eight hours per day. As we CSOs worked with the Inspectors in the international passenger area, their job seemed to appeal to those of us who wished to spend more time with wives and family. Unlike the Customs Agents who were expected to be mobile and move from location to location, Inspectors could stay at one port of entry for their entire career if they wished.

Most of the Customs Inspectors at the newly opened Dulles International Airport were veteran Customs Inspectors who had transferred from New York. They had learned their skills from the most talented Inspectors who had developed a knack for spotting individuals who were lying while declaring their overseas acquisitions. Although there wasn't a formal name for these skills at the time, they would later become known as behavioral profiling in which the Inspector is taught to observe small physiological changes in the individual as he or she answers questions. These include pulsing of the veins in the neck, rapid blinks or eye movements, looking away from the questioner, and many other subtle changes or movements. Some Customs Inspectors have an uncanny ability to detect if someone is carrying contraband after one question or just a careful glance. These are the same skills that security officers questioning departing passengers must develop. They must be trained and their skills honed, through constant use with other more experienced officers.

At this time, Customs was beginning to develop automated databases that allowed Inspectors to check a name against a list of known or suspected smugglers.

Before this primitive automated system, we simply Had paper notices or lookouts giving pictures of suspects or new modes of smuggling. Today the upon system has been developed into a true integrated passengers system with the Immigration and Naturalization scrutiny a Service, the FBI's National Crime Information intensive System, and the DEA' NADIS system. Passenger names are entered by the airline at the point of are embarkation for the US directly or through passport readers. When a passenger deplanes, Customs knows traveling if he or she is someone who needs special attention. Customs Inspectors are trained to never directly confirm if an individual's name is in the database of reasons suspect individuals. They may write a letter to Customs Headquarters and attempt to obtain that larger information but that are many clauses in the Freedom of Information Act which can be cited to refuse to divurge the information.

For many years, the airlines berated Customs for that som not adopting the red/green system in effect throughout Europe in which the passenger selects a line if he has search something to declare and if not, he or she passes through Customs with only the possibility of a spot or random stop to answer questions. The Customs search Inspectors rightly believed that they should confront each passenger and ask a few questions to see if any of the answers or behavioral characteristics justified a more detailed search or questioning.

Another area of concern and great public interest over the past few years has been the existence of and use of profiles. The Customs Service has been the target of a number of law suits and complaints by Afro-American officers that profiles have been misused to target Afro-American passengers for intensive examinations. There is no doubt that based upon a past pattern of drug seizures, certain passengers from certain destinations are given more scrutiny and thereby more pat-downs or other types of intensive searches. For example, Jamaica and Nigeria are two countries in which drugs are readily available and the number of seizures indicate that persons traveling to those areas have easy access to them and may bring them back. A large number of Afro Americans also travel to these destinations for many reasons including tourism, business and pleasure. A combination of these two facts will bring about a large number of searches due to the suspicions of the Inspectors even thought there is no specific information about a particular passenger. The problem is that some Customs supervisors along with individual inspectors were not doing their duty and justifying the search with specific factors. It was easier to skip the step of looking for the one or two individuals with suspicious stories or budgets in their clothing and just search as many as possible with the hopes of getting a seizure. Customs move to address this problem by instituting more requirements to document the specific factors which led to the search and putting the responsibility on the supervisors on duty to personally approve the intensive examination.

There are a number of degrees in an intensive examination. The most unobstrusive is the pat down to verify if a object is hidden under clothing. The next would be a request to open or remove certain items of clothing in a secure search room. The final would be a full strip search with possible body cavity examination if there is sufficient justification to suspect a body carry. The most vexing problem is the ingestion of narcotics in sealed balloons or condums or their insertion inside body cavities. Customs does not have the authority to force someone to undergo an x-ray or a probe within the body without the consent of the individual being searched or a court order. The tactics which have evolved is to detain the suspect for a reasonable amount of time in a special facility or trailer in the expection that the contraband will be passed from the body. The individual is offered food and water and he or she is made aware that it the contraband is released within the body if may not be possible to save the person's life. Usually this pressure is sufficient to get their consent for x-rays or the use of laxatives. The "mule" or individual carrying the contraband is someone in desperate need of money or who has been coerced in someway to carry the deadly substance within the body. There are several tragic stories of those who did not get to a hospital in time and died a horrible death.

The third primary field component of the Customs Service was and is the Import Specialist. They focus on the commercial business of Customs and process the paperwork (today almost completely automated and paperless), which is submitted to enter foreign goods into the commerce of the United States. These individuals were located in the Customs House or main Customs office for each port of entry and verified that the goods were properly classified in the Tariff Schedule and that the correct value was listed in the proper duties and taxes were calculated. We had little exposure to this element of the Customs mission and few of the CSOs became Import Specialists. As I was to learn later, there was a large cadre of other positions in the commercial side of Customs including entry personnel, attorneys, chemists, etc.

As is the case in other agencies of the US Government such as the Immigration and Naturalization Service, Customs has the dual role of enforcement and trade facilitation. At times these two distinct missions meshed smoothly and the official line of Customs is that the missions are complementary. Facilitation of low risk individuals and cargo allows the agency to focus its attention on the small number of high-risk shipments.

In practice, it doesn't work this smoothly. The Agency either has a focus on enforcement or facilitation depending upon the philosophy of the Administration and the Commissioner of Customs at the time. During my time as a CSO in the Nixon administration, when the Commissioner was Myles Ambrose, there was a clear emphasis on enforcement. The Agency was willing to antagonize some of the business community including brokers and airlines in order to achieve greater enforcement results. In later administrations, this emphasis was reversed and if an officer attempted to do too much in terms of searches and seizures, the word quickly came down to ease up.

In 1971, Customs was a relatively small Bureau within the Department of Treasury. The total number of employees was five or six thousand and it seemed as if everyone knew each other. Most employees spent their whole government career with Customs and were generally very pleased with their jobs and the Agency. The Customs Security Officer program with over 2000 new employees was the greatest increase in personnel that Customs had ever received. This expansion of personnel and in the scope of the mission of the Agency started the process to convert Customs into a far different entity with a workforce of almost 20, 000 today with a fleet of aircraft and boats with sophisticated computers and other technology.

As is the case in other areas of government functions, there is an ongoing rivalry and competition for scarce resources and publicity on enforcement law matters and Customs is a participant in this friendly even and sometimes not so friendly contest. In the specific area of narcotics enforcement, Customs is in competition with DEA and to some extent the FBI. In some areas such as warrant-less searches at the border, Customs has the clear legal authority and is the lead agency. However, DEA controls the intelligence overseas through its Attaché offices in key narcotics supply and transit countries and has been known to withhold information in order to make a major seizure once the narcotics have crossed the border and entered into the United States. Without good intelligence, Customs faces the mind-bending task of determining which of the thousands of vehicles and containers entering the US every day contain contraband. Technology such as large x-ray units help and the Customs detector dogs do a wonderful job but it is still looking for a needle in a haystack. We used to guess that we apprehended approximately 10% of the drugs crossing the border but this was just a guess based upon estimates of crop production and reports on drugs on the streets.

The competition for large-scale narcotic seizures got even hotter during the 1980s and 90s with the asset forfeiture laws. Agencies were able to seize all the assets associated with a narcotics case including cars, boats, houses, land and planes, not to mention bank accounts here and abroad. These funds could just be used to pay informants, buy equipment and offset other Jaw enforcement costs. The monies could also be shared with state and local authorities and overseas law enforcement agencies and this could be used to get even better support and intelligence from these groups.

At the borders there are three border inspection agencies that are often confused with one another by the infrequent traveler. Customs and the Immigration and Naturalization Service (INS) are the two largest and the Department of Agriculture has its Animal, Plant and Quarantine officers to guard against dangers to our food supply. Customs and INS were and still are at war on a constant basis. At the land borders, we use a primary and secondary system in which an Inspector From one agency does the initial inquiry and enters the name or licensed tags into the automated system (now known as the integrated border inspection system or IBIS).

Both agencies along with Agriculture man secondary stations and any one suspected of a violation is routed to the appropriate secondary location for a more detailed inspection. Sounds good in theory, but it did not work so well in practice. Customs always accused INS of not doing its share the primary booths and putting extra burdens on Customs, which reduced our ability to man our secondary booths. Also, each agency did not believe that the other paid enough attention to their needs during the primary interview. Customs wanted narcotic seizures and INS wanted illegal immigrants.

There was even less cooperation at the airports and both agencies had their own officers to do a two-step system in which arriving passengers had to pass through both an immigration screening and a Customs screening.

There were numerous efforts by various administrations and the Congress to unify the border inspection process into a seamless single agency effort.

However, efforts to create a single border inspection agency failed repeatedly due to the unions the from each agency, the agency leadership on both sides, the Congressional backers of each agency, and the private sector, which had to deal with each agency. The merger of both Customs and INS into the new Department of Homeland Security should solve the problem, but at the cost of losing the long histories and traditions of both agencies.

All of us at Customs were very proud of the long history of Customs, and we worried that Customs would lose its identity as a small part of a much larger bureaucracy.

We felt it could be more difficult to keep the special esprit and dedication of the workforce.

One issue, which was settled shortly after the demise of the Sky Marshal program, was the Border patrol and Customs Patrol issue. Both agencies asserted the right to patrol the land between authorized ports of entry; Customs looking for the smugglers of f contraband, and the INS Border Patrol for the smugglers of people. In reality the smugglers often did both in using the illegal immigrants to bring narcotics into the United States. Finally the Congress and the Executive Branch agreed that there should be a single Border Patrol under INS with responsibility for all illegal activity between ports of entry. This has worked well over the years especially since Customs began to focus on air interdiction and small boats.

On the sea and to a lesser extent, in the air, the Customs Service shares jurisdiction with the Coast Guard. The Coast Guard and Customs were both part of the Department of Treasury until the Department of Transportation was created in 1964.and they are under the same jurisdiction today. In most instances Coast Guard and Customs work well together in the air an marine environment although the Customs Service uses fast interception boats in the inshore waters. Th larger Coast Guard vessels are used in the open waters and careful coordination is required to avoid disasters.

The debate over the Department of Homeland Security is an example of the difficulties in combining Federal agencies with a long history of competition and with distinct feelings towards the personnel and actions of other agencies. Is not an easy or painless process.

As we CSOs at Dulles performed our first tour of row ground duty, many of us were beginning to make in the decisions about our future in Customs. There were already rumblings that the CSO program would have a limited lifespan. A number of us did not relish resuming the lengthy flights, hours of boredom and nights in hotel rooms across the world. The initial glamour had faded and it was becoming a job more than an adventure.

Since there were relatively few departing aircraft at Dulles, most of us were asked to assist the Customs called Inspectors in the processing of passengers arriving from overseas. We begin to work more closely with the Inspectors and learned the tricks of their trade and the life of the Inspector. The Chief Inspector was a big scary Irishman from the docks of New York. He had white hair and a massive face with bloodshoot eyes from too many drinks on late nights in the bars. We soon learned that he was not a man you wished to cross but that he was a wonderful incentive to convince a smuggler that he or she must confess or face some horrible treatment in the back room.

That Spring in Dulles, the work that I did in the International arrivals area with the Inspectors helped me to decide on my career in Customs. I begin to learn the traits and personalities of the individual Inspectors and to truly appreciate their skills and humor. Dulles had only a few scheduled Pan Am and TWA flights per day but was a primary diversion airport when JFK or Logan became overburdened or closed due to inclement weather. Some of the Inspectors related stories of Working over 60 days in a row and making massive amounts of overtime money in the winter when the westher was bad or in the summer when the charter flights failed the skies. There was a brotherhood among the Inspectors that I relish had not experienced before in Customs. They were enforcement officers but allowed to be represented by a Union which protected them somewhat against arbitrary management actions or transfers. The overtime money paid for by the airlines who required the overtime services was quite good. If you were called back to work in the night you received a half day's pay and then another quarter day's pay two hour period of time(or less). It was much better than double time and any work on Sunday basically guaranteed you two days pay. T here were stories of Inspectors making more money than the Commissioner himself. Later this was all changed and salary caps were put in to avoid the large amounts of overtime paid out.

At Dulles, most of Afro-Americans most of the Inspectors and a were charming Irish Jewish individual from New York who was a for-mer jewelry store owner and collector of antiques. All had wonderful stories of New York and the history of Customs. It was a custom to play cards in the back search and locker rooms while waiting for flights to arrive late at night. The card game of choice was Hearts and the games were full of intrigue and strategy. We had certain Inspectors who specialized in "shooting the moon" or talking all 26 points and thereby giving the other players 26 points against them while receiving none themselves. The stakes for winning were never more than a few dollars, but it was a game of Honor and everyone tried to give the current leaders the point in order to prolong the game until the end.

The veteran Inspectors from New York gave us many examples of never taking anyone or anything for granted. There were famous stories in JFK of the pregnant lady who really had a fake stomach with kilos of heroin hidden inside or the Priest who was carrying a fortune in stolen gems into the country. The Cardinal rule was to always verify your initial feeling about a person by asking a series of questions about the person's trip and activities. As you listen to the responses to the questions, you would get a feeling about the person and if everything held together. One slip or an answer which did not fit the image of the person before you whose grounds for more questions and perhaps more intensive search.

In working with Inspectors, I began to gain a better under-standing of human character and the strange things people did to try to beat the system and bring something illegal into the country or to cheat the government of a few dollars of Customs duty. I would like to relate some of the strange incidents that I observed or was involved in during this time of ground duty.

Ira was a Inspector who prided himself both as a ladies man and someone who could always find a restricted item on a person. He often said that most people attempted to beat the system in some way and that he could tell in a moment if was trying to scam him. One of the funniest episodes involving him was a demure lady with many pieces of luggage returning from a trip to Paris. She was visibily and vocally upside that Ira was going through her baggage including her undies. We could tell that Ira was getting a little peeved also by all of her complaints and indignation. He kept asking her if she was sure that she had declared everything that she had acquired overseas. She kept denying that she had purchased anything. Finally Ira felt some-thing in her bag and proudly held it up for all the nearby passengers to see. "Lady, this item was definitely purchased in Paris and you did not declare it." It was a massive dildo that caused the lady to blush all the colors of the rainbow and the passengers to break into laughter. I am sure that she never smuggled any item again.

Another incident involved one of the few female Inspectors on duty at Dulles. There were only two and one of them soon moved to another job. The remaining lady was a former Police officer from Denver who did not take any sass from anyone. She prided herself as being tougher than most of the males and perhaps she had to adopt that attitude to survive in a mostly male environment. "R" also did not like airline stewardesses and often gave them a rough time in questionning them and searching their bags. On one late charter flight, one of the stewardesses was black and she was either tired or had a bad attitudes herself towards any enforcement person particularly white females. "R" told the supervisor that she believed the stewardess was smuggling some type of contraband probably grass or hash and that it was hiddened under her clothing. She was given permission to conduct a personal search in the searchroom.

R was the only female officer on duty that night but we authorized our female cashier to go with her into the search room. Several of us waited outside the room just to be near in case something developed, The searchroom had a panic light connected to a concealed button inside so if anything went wrong, we could intervene. Shortly after they went into the room, we had some horrible screams and noises from inside and will t he outside light went on. We rushed into the room and what a sight! The poor cashier was standing in the corner crying as "R" and the stewardess rolled around on the floor. We did not know what to grab to separate them as blouses and hair was being pulled and curses were filling the room. We grabbed what every we could to separate them and allowed everyone to get their clothes back on. "R" accused the stewardess of assulting a federal office while the stewardess accused "R" of inappropriately touching certain parts of her body. No drugs or contraband were found and I believe all charges on both sides were eventually dropped. All the old time Inspectors told us that the most dangerous event we would ever be involved in was a cat fight!

Another common occurrence was the smuggling of cuban cigars which were readily available in every part of the world except the U.S. A. Invariably someone would attempt to bring some of the cigars back hidden inside their shoes, toilet kit or underware. We would find them and allow the individuals to sign a consent document for their destruction in lieu of paying a fine and having us formally seize them. Of course the passengers were quite irrate and often accused us of taking the cigars to smoke ourselves. One particular individual in a late night flight was particularly upset with a seizure of his priced cigars. He grabbed them out of the Inspector's hand and personally ground them up in his hands and threw them on the floor. We made him pick them up and his name went into our database someone who had willfully disobeyed the instructions of a law enforcement officer.

Flights from Germany were a specific problem due to the desired German nationals to pick a prized piece of sausage or "wurst" into the United States for their own consumption or to give to a dear friend in the States. There was and still is a danger of numerous diseases being carried in untreated meats from Europe. Rindapest and hoof and mouth deceased could devastate our livestock. We had Department of Agriculture Inspectors working with us but the Customs Inspectors were the first line of defense to confiscate the forbidden meat. Little old ladies would go to extremes in their attempts to smuggle the delicacy past the Customs Inspectors. We found them hidden up dressees, strapped to their legs and in every possible place of concealment in luggage. And the wailing that took place when we discovered them and took them away. It sounded as if we were taking their first born child away from them.

In the early 70's LSD, Marijuana and hashish were the primary drugs so we're smuggled into the country. We would get an occasional heroin seizure but that was mainly controlled by the Mafia in New York and was not normally done by amateurs. Cocaine was unknown at the time. Of course, We had the normal profiles of grass and hashed users. Usually younger "hippy" types coming from the Middle East or Southwest Asia. Usually the amount we seized at Dulles were small. I made my first marijuana seizure from a young man from Africa who was carrying a wooden game board about 3 or 4 inches thick. It felt too heavy and we took it apart and found about 5 pounds of grass. LSD tabs were harder to find since they were often just on slips of paper.

Later in my career in Customs, the amounts we only were seizing from passengers in the 70's seemed totally insignificant. In my tenure as Assistant District Director of Inspection and Control in the Tampa District, one of our Inspectors on duty supervising the I had uplading of a cargo ship from Honduras spotted some individuals paying too much attention to a shipment of Hondurian hardwood lumber. He called our Countraband Enforcement Team who drilled the lumber and it tested positive for cocaine. The next two Customs Agents and DEA were notified and set up Program surveillance with hidden cameras. They trailed the lumber shipment to a suspected dealer in Tarpon Springs and made the bust

As they were taking the packets of cocaine out of the hidden compartments in the hardwood. The total was over 8000 pounds which was a record at the time which has since been surpassed many times as I mentioned before, the long, late hours of the Inspectors took their toll on individuals. Marriages broke up due to too many nights alone for the spouse and the constant possiblity of love affairs at the airport between the Inspectors and various airline and airport personnel. There were usually two or three affairs going on at any one time and of course, the secrets of the lovers leaked out to everyone and the gossip spread quickly. Some of the Inspectors would visit the airport bar after long shifts of work and this also contributed to a number of late night wrecks along the Dulles toll road as sleepy, and somewhat intoxicated Inspectors tried to drive home late at night.

I was married to Louise in July 1971 and we had only a three-day honeymoon in Virginia Beach before I had to leave for New York to begin my next two months of flight duty. She had to move into our apartment in Falls Church with the help of her family. I had already sent a letter to the Customs personnel Office asking to be considered for any Customs Inspector vacancy in Dulles and, although I did not know it when I began flying again out of JFK. These next two months would be my last in the Sky Marshal Program.

Chapter 7

MOMENTS OF HIGH ANXIETY AND STRANGE OCCURRENCES

I RETURNED TO flight duty after a three-day honeymoon with a growing realization that I needed to begin to look for another occupation within Customs to avoid the long days of travel away from my new wife. Little did I realize that my one moment of high anxiety as a Sky Marshal was approaching.

I was flying with one partner on a 707 from JFK to Lisbon, Portugal. I was in first class trying to keep awake by reading a murder suspense novel. Dinner had been served and most of the passengers in first class had turned off their reading lights and were attempting to get a little sleep before we arrived in Lisbon.

Suddenly, a young male of possible Arabic extraction came through the curtains from economy into first class. I was sitting in the last row of first class and as he quickly brushed past me on the way to the front of the cabin I was momentarily shocked and came to full alertness. As the individual reached the small front cocktail lounge on the 707 where the flight crew were sitting and talking, they quickly stopped the man and explained that he could not move from economy to first class and that he needed to return to his seat.

I was fully alert now and realized that this might be an actual skyjacking underway. I quickly drew my revolver and rested it in my lap. In my mind I decided that if he attempted to go to the pilot door or threatened the flight crew in any way, I was going to say "Stop" once, and if he did not obey, shoot him. I began to edge forward in the darkened cabin, the man apparently did not understand English well and after a moment of discussion turned and headed towards the pilot's door. I was now in a cold sweat and begin to raise my gun and to go forward towards him. Part of my brain could not believe that his was actually happening but the other part was quickly calculating angles of fires and preparing for the noise of a shot in an enclosed space. I began raising my arm to aim directly for a shot into the man's spine from about 10 feet away.

The flight attendants grabbed the arm of the man as he attempted to go forward and told him that he must not go that way. Finally he muttered that he was sick and had to go to the toilet. They let him go into the first class toilet and he quickly vomited into the toilet bowl. He was simply sick to his stomach and first confused about the location of the toilet.

I quietly returned the gun to my holster and sat and down. I was soaked with sweat and shaking, realizing that I had almost accidentally killed someone. After the man finished throwing up, he was escorted back into the economy cabin. The rest of the flight was from uneventful but all of a sudden I began to realize that the unexpected could happen at any time. As they say in law enforcement, hours of boredom and then lit be seconds of pure panic.

This was my one and only near event in the Sky Marshal program. Over the years in correspondence with other former Sky Marshals directly and through the Sky Marshal Association and its reunions held in New York, I was able to learn of the other high and low points of the other Sky Marshals' careers.

The following are some of the personal stories of other Sky Marshals. I have not given their real names and in some cases, the stories are second-hand and cannot be authenticated.

Sky Marshal EF:

I never made an arrest or stopped a skyjacking on any of my flights, although I did the former and possibly the latter while on ground duty in JFK.

However, a partner and I did save two people's lives. But, as with most of my CSO adventures, this happened during a layover between flights. be It happened during a three-day layover in Karachi during a Pan Am around the world flight from JFK to gr Bangkok. As many of our colleagues had done before us, my partner and I hired the infamous Captain Charlie and his dhow for a day of fishing, eating, drinking beer, swimming and other pleasures under the sun of the Arabian Gulf. My partner was a CSO from Baltimore who name has disappeared over the years. With us came part of a crew from Southern Cross Airways, a small charter airline based in Kuala Lumpur, Malaysia; the captain and flight engineer, who were furloughed from Pan Am, a steward who was a Malaysian Moslem, and a stewardess who was a non-Muslim Malaysian Chinese. My partner and I had conflicting amorous plans for her.

The sun and the beer had gotten too hot, and the fishing was too cold, so we all decided to go for a swim. However, as soon as we got into the water, we realized that the current was running so fast that we would never be able to swim back to the boat. So we yelled to Captain Charlie to come and pick us up and just floated and paddled, lazily enjoying the warm water. After about five minutes, the Steward calmly announced: "I can't swim any more," and we and started to sink. I was closest to him so I grabbed him and kept him afloat. Two minutes later, the Stewardess made the same announcement and my partner grabbed her.

What had started out as a pleasant swim in exotic waters had now become very serious because most this people who are in danger of drowning eventually begin to struggle wildly. With Captain Charlie's boat nowhere in sight, my partner and I decided to make a grab for the anchor line of the last dhow within reach, since their crew had ignored our cries for help. But we could not reach it. Our last hope was an auto tire hanging as a bumper from the middle of the dhow. I told the steward to swim or thrash; let go of him, and SO made a last desperate grab for the tire, which I barely the managed to seize. I stretched my foot out to the steward who grabbed on for dear life. And my partner managed to grab onto the steward with one hand. There we remained until Captain Charlie—whose anchor had been stuck and had to be cut loose—finally picked us up.

I know the cliché that the secret to success is to be in the right place at the right time. My partner refused to confirm or deny that cliché the next morning. I have heard, however, that Captain Charlie was one arrested, executed, murdered, or all of the above for his role in the narcotics trade. I do not know if this is true.

Sky Marshal B.H.:

I was a correction officer in Riker's Island. While waiting for dinner, I read in the paper that the test for pay "Sky Marshal" was to be given at Varick Street in New York. I walked into the warden's office and we dropped my tin on the desk and said the equivalent of: "It's been real and it's been fun, but it hasn't been real on th fun." I took the test on Monday and received a call on Wednesday that I had the job. I said that I couldn't report because I was going hunting. The caller said to come in when I got back. I knew then that I had found the job of all jobs. I graduated from Class Three at TASOS.

Enough of that. Here are some things that I recall: I don't remember the officer who was shot in the leg at Pan Am, but he jumped some nut to prevent him from shooting Tony P. of Pan Am security, also took a shot at the perp but this one wasn't well known.

I was in London and one of my many flights there. I got to the airport for my flight. At the jetway, I realized I had left my gun in the Customs office. I made my way back but couldn't make my flight. I called JFK and was told to pick up a flight as the partner of a Special Agent who was coming in the next day. I was also told to report to one of the Special Agents in charge of CSOs when I returned. I did, no one remembered why, and I conveniently had no idea why I had been called in. It was a great job indeed.

I was also in London when they switched to base 10 from their former currency. I ordered a meal at the hotel and when the bill came, it looked like a small mortgage. I noticed the staff looking at me. I spent the next few minutes explaining the simplicity of base 10 and simple addition with decimals. I still had to pay for my meal.

I was in Beirut talking with the security people. We were talking police trash and showing off our issued firearms. I noticed a pair of cuffs in a glass case on the wall. They were large and medieval-looking, A real set of mega irons. When I returned to pick up my weapon, I noticed the cuffs were out of the case and being worn by a prisoner. While the officer and I were talking, The door opened and in walks a slim individual, holding a cigarette in his fingers, palm up. His suit was fitted snugly and his looked as if he had stepped off of the set of "Casablanca". I looked in the leg around for Bogart and Bacall. Everyone in the room jumped to their feet and stood braced at attention. The prisoner looked as if he would die of fright. I knew that the individual who just walked into the room had the power of life and death over the prisoner and, for all I knew, everyone else. A great appreciation of the freedoms we enjoy in America washed over me. We don't know how fortunate we are to be born in the USA.

I was in LA for a layover. I developed a fever and was treating it with aspirin every four hours. I stayed in bed all day and night. You know that a minor earthquake chose that night to make its presence felt. Stuff car fell from the shelves and the bed bounced around, but apart from cracks, no damage was done and I flew out the next day. I went to Shannon Airport in Ireland right after St. his Patrick was demoted. I asked if Mr. Patrick's day was still celebrated. They not amused. The ugly American strikes again.

I was in New Delhi with my partner, C.D. He wanted to buy some gemstones for his wife and got the name of a place where he could get a deal. He talked me into going with him. He stopped a rickshaw and showed him the address. He took us to places I knew we would never get out of on our own. We had gone back into time to the 1930s. We got to a shop and were escorted into a back room. I whispered to C.D., telling him that, if we got out of this place alive, I would never go anywhere with him again.

This character comes over and spreads these stones want on a pad. C.D. picks some, the guy weighs them on a hand held balance and C. D. pays.

Obviously we got back, and true to my word, I never went shopping with Carl again.

It was the best job I've ever had and I emotionally keep a bag packed, ready to fly at a moment's notice.

Sky Marshall B.D.:

On a flight from Seattle to Honolulu in the summer of 1971, three of us Sky Marshals arrived at the car rental desk at the airport. Sky Marshal "Ted" is the last to arrive at the counter. Later at a hotel where the three of us were staying, an employee from the rental car company shows up with an athletic bag that was left at the rental car counter at the airport. In the bag, which belonged to Ted, were his badge, ID. and his loaded .38 revolver. Grateful Ted was reunited with his equipment.

Another incident also involved Ted. He went to his room in a hotel in Chicago after a flight. Ted settled down to watch some TV and, while watching the tube, he decides to dry-fire his .38. Ted methodically emptied his weapon and placed the bullets in a drawer adjacent to the TV and his seat. Ted heard a knock at the door while he was dry-firing his weapon. He quickly reloaded his weapon, concealed it and opened the door.

The maid was there waiting to make up the bed. Ted told her to go ahead and resumed watching TV.

He refrained from dry-firing his weapon as he didn't stones want to frighten the maid. She left a few minutes later. Ted took his weapon out of its place of concealment and commences to dry fire.

Oops! Ted fired one shot through the TV. He forgot that he had reloaded his weapon. He lost his job shortly after this incident was reported.

Sky marshal X
(several sources but no one admits direct involvement):

One of our ex-marine Sky Marshals had a well-developed reputation as a hothead who would always get into confrontations. On a trip to Paris, he and his Partner got a French taxi driver to take them to a dingy bar somewhere on the left bank. After many hours of drinking with some pretty dangerous looking characters, Sky Marshal X got into a heated argument with one of the patrons of the bar who had a sleek Peugeot parked outside. No one remembers what started the argument; but eventually Sky Marshal X was thrown out. He then took out a knife that he was carrying illegally on his flights and punctured the four tires of the Peugeot in plain sight of everyone still in the bar. The gendarmes were called and he ended up in the Parisian jail for the night. Needless to say, he was quickly booted from the service when he finally was returned to the US.

Sky Marshal R.N.:

In the winter of 1971/72, I was flying "tail end Charlie" on a TWA 747 from Frankfurt, Germany, to JFK. The aircraft was in the final approach and I had prepared for landing by putting my gear in my m briefcase. By gear, I mean my Model 60 S&W .38 he special revolver, my handcuffs, and my blackjack. On my person, I was only carrying my credentials and a be Colt .45 semi-automatic pistol in a shoulder hostler under my jacket. The aircraft was just about to touch the runway when one of the flight attendants approached from to behind me and exclaimed "come quickly, they need you in the rear". I hustled to the rear along the starboard aisle but I could see nothing except startled to passengers. That meant that whatever was occurring was taking place in the rear cross passageway where my vision was obstructed by the bulkhead. All that I could think was that I was going to take action with an unauthorized weapon and even worse, fire it.

When I got to the passageway, I found a young man struggling with the Director Customer Service (a glorified purser). I flashed my credentials, identified myself and him to cease and desist, which he did. I asked the "DCS" if he wanted the man arrested for interfering with a member of the flight crew in the up performance of their duties. He said he did; so I read the man his rights and placed him under arrest.

When one deplanes at JFK from an international flight, you go down an escalator and enter an area separated by a large glass wall, which separates the waiting room from the international arrival area. With this in mind, the young man asked me not to handcuff him as his parents would be seeing him arrive and any, to would be considerably disturbed. Actually, there was no way that I could cuff him as my cuffs were back in in my seat and there was a mob of passengers between here and there pushing to get off of the aircraft. However, I played it cool and told him that if he would s and a behave, I would agree to his request.

We deplaned, waves were exchanged and we proceeded thru Immigration and Customs to the runway Customs office where we awaited the party from TWA to prefer charges. I asked the prisoner if he wanted to talk about what had happened. It turned out that he was a GI returning to the States after completing his tour of duty in West Germany. The flight attendants had sold him cocktails until he was somewhat inebriated. He needed to relieve himself; so he decided to make his way in his befuddled state to the lavatory even though the fasten seat belt light had gone on and the aircraft was landing. A female flight attendant got up from her seat and tried to stop him, but cursing her, he pushed her aside. He was then confronted by the "DCS" and they started fighting and that is when I was called. I might add that the TWA flight crew except for the part about him being served too many cocktails confirmed his story.

The end of the story is that TWA declined to press charges, the man was "unarrested", one of he cabin attendants returned my briefcase to me with all of my gear intact, and I vowed never to separate myself from my equipment again since, when the whistle blows you go with what you have.

My name was "Four gun" although I really never carried more than three. I think that the statute of limitations has expired so they cannot get me for carrying unauthorized weapons.

Another story from R.N.:

I was overnighting with a young CSO from 1 Philadelphia in Frankfurt. He wanted to go out on the town for some nightlife and he particularly wished to and visit a bar he had been told had the most beautiful young ladies in Germany. I told him to enjoy himself but be careful about buying drinks for the "young ladies". I warned him that they were paid to get all unwary men to buy them expensive drinks and they drank non-alcoholic libations while the man was drinking and paying top dollar. He looked at me but didn't really understand what I was trying to tell him. Later that night the first young lady asked him to buy her a drink and gave him a coy smile and promises of later favors. Of course, he bought her the drink while looking at her blond hair and blue eyes. When the drink arrived, the large burly bartender told him that it was $20 a drink. By the end of the night he had spent his salary check for the next month. Live and learn!

Another time, a partner from New York left his Model 60 S&W on the toilet of a TWA 747. One of the stewardesses found it and returned it to him with a smile. Another CSO actually dropped his gun down the toilet hole. It was a Colt with the 2 inch barrel and somehow it went down through the hole into the storage tank below. I don't know how they finally got it out. It is an easy thing to do when unbuckling your pants. I dropped a handcuff key down the hole one time.

Sky Marshall W.R:

I flew domestic flights primarily on Eastern airlines. One of my partners was a little overweight and did not wish to use a shoulder holster for his Colt Detective with a 2 inch barrel. He has also replaced the standard grips on his revolver with special ones that did not have the little hook on the end, which allowed the revolver to be hooked on a belt.

We were on a flight from JFK to San Juan on a 747. It was a hot flight and was usually very crowded. None of us wore suits or sport coats since this was not the typical dress for someone going to San Juan. My partner simply put his Colt in the waistband of his pants and pulled his shirt out and over his belt to conceal his weapon. The two of us were in first class and a third CSO was in economy. The 747 had a cocktail lounge up top and we alternated being upstairs and down in the main cabin. I came down the circular ladder and he was supposed to go up top to replace me while I stayed downstairs. He stood up to stretch and suddenly his Colt slipped down his pants and landed with a loud clunk on the cabin floor. A number of the passenger looked at him and the gun in horror and immediately started pressing their call buttons for assistance. The quick-thinking flight attendant picked up the intercom microphone and assured everyone that my partner was in fact a Sky Marshal and they had nothing to fear. My partner picked up his gun and with a red face took his seat. So much for his undercover role on that flight.

A second and potentially more serious incident took place on the New York/ Miami/Chicago run on Eastern. This flight had been hijacked in the past and we were always alert for someone seeking to take over and fly to Cuba.

In our preflight meetings with the flight crew, we had informed them that if they noticed anything suspicious, they should write a note, put it into a magazine and give it to us as reading material.

I was in the first class section of a 747 with my partner again. The flight was going smoothly and I was anticipating a layover in Miami and getting some time in the sun. To my horror, one of the stewardesses walked to me and asked me if I would like to read an article in a magazine. With trembling hands, I opened the magazine hoping against hope that I would not find a message inside, but it was there. The note said that one of the passengers had a small bag in his hands and would not put it down for a second to eat or drink. The passenger was very nervous and seemed to be sweating heavily. She gave me his seat number. I looked up the aisle and saw that there was a vacant seat immediately behind the suspect passenger. I moved to that seat and watched him closely. Sure enough the small bag that he held tightly could be a weapon or an explosive. He was definitely nervous acting strangely. My partner had also been notified and he told the crew to call ahead to Miami and have the police meet us upon landing.

In the meantime, I touched the grip of my revolver and hoped that nothing would happen. We landed safely at Miami International and the police came into the aircraft to assist us. We grabbed the individual and asked him what he was hiding in the bag. It turned out to be his family jewels that he was taking to his family and he was afraid of being robbed. That one flight aged me ten years.

Sky Marshal E.F.:

It was early in the morning on a Pan Am flight from Rome to Ankara to Teheran, which was always considered high risk. A very nervous young man, of distinctly Middle Eastern appearance, walked from economy into first class where I was sitting, and asked the purser if he could visit the cockpit. She told him no, but he insisted. She said that she would ask the captain, a delaying tactic that usually meant one of the flight crew would come out of the cockpit and make sure that he returned to his seat, using force if that in became necessary. Our instructions were to keep our cover in this sort of situation unless it became clear that a skyjacking was taking place or passengers or crew were in danger. The flight engineer, a huge man who could have carried the man back to his seat with one hand if it had been necessary, came out of the cockpit and got the same refusal from the passenger and had the same response as the purser. He would ask the captain and he disappeared back into the cockpit. The passenger had moved up close to the cockpit door, so I picked up a magazine and moved up to the circular lounge seat, which on the Pan Am 707s of that era was located not far behind the cockpit door.

The engineer re-emerged from the cockpit, and to my horror, he said: "The captain says it's OK."

The engineer moved out of the passenger's way, which, in the narrow spaces on the 707 put him squarely between the passenger and me. To this day, I cannot recall whether I went around, over, under or through the flight engineer. But I did arrive immediately behind the passenger with my gun pointed at his back and my finger on the trigger, just as he took one step into the cockpit and stopped.

It seemed like forever but I know it was only a few seconds before he had seen his fill, and turned around and returned to his seat. He never knew who close that flight came to being his last because I had pretended to be interested in seeing the cockpit too, and had kept my gun concealed under the magazine I had been pretending to read. But the ashen complexion of the business traveler I had been chatting with before the incident started showed that he knew how close to something terrible we all had come.

Sky marshal shootings:

There were at least two incidents in which CSOs were engaged in shooting. One incident took place off duty in a New York Bar. Apparently, an off-duty police officer and a CSO were trying to pick up the same woman in a bar and guns were drawn and shots exchanged. The CSO was fired.

The other incident took place at JFK during predeparture searches and a CSO and an airport security officer were wounded in a gun battle with an ex-con who was attempting to take a weapon on a plane.

Sky Marshal E.R:

I was on a TWA 707 flight to Geneva with a 45minute stop over in Zurich.

My partner (he never made it through his first year, something in his background caught up with him) was in first class and I was in the far back.

The curtain between the two sections was closed.

The TWA stewardesses were a bit older than I. (I was 23 at the time). But, on this flight, there was one fairly young gal working in the back. Well, believe me, with no green light from me, she starts getting real friendly.

Every time she walked by, she would bump me, stick her wet finger in my ear, pull my hair (I had some then), etc.

After dinner and the movie, lights started going out and lots of folks started going to sleep, including the guy next to me. So now, there is little or no activity in the whole plane. So I am reading some novel and this stewardess comes up to me, hands me a magazine and says: "Sir, here is the magazine you requested."

Right then and there, I knew my life was over!! Something bad must have happened up in first class behind that curtain and I was sure we were on our way to some far away destination. Because I remembered in school, the instructors said a really good way to get a message to your partner was by using a magazine with the message inside. Well, the stewardess had awakened the guy next to me when she delivered the magazine, either that or my heart pounding so fast and so loud had awakened him. Anyway, as nonchalantly as possible, I started thumbing through the magazine looking for the dreaded note out of view of my nosey neighbor. I would turn a couple of pages, look up at the curtain and then turn a few more pages.

I fully expected to see armed individuals walk back to where I was seated and take me away.

To make a long story short, I finally came across a TWA cocktail napkin inside the magazine, unfolded it, and it says: "I love you."

Well my partner was a guy so I knew it wasn't from him. It was from the young stewardess who had been sticking her finger in my ear! My first thoughts were to kill her! My second thought was to see just how serious she was. So during our brief stop in Zurich, I asked her if she wanted to go out to dinner when we arrived in Geneva. She didn't say Yes and she didn't say no. I never saw her again—But will never forget the "anguish" she put me through.

Sky Marshal R. G. N.:

My partner and I deadheaded on a TWA flight to Tarabolos Airport in Tripoli, Libya on a short flight from Madrid. I think TWA flew into Libya only once a week. The passengers were mainly oil well technicians.

"Well", the Captain said. "We will see you in town" and we headed to Libyan Immigration only to be told that since we didn't have visas we would not be let into the country. They said that they had told TWA that they were tired of bending their rules and letting security police in every week without visas. So what could we do? The TWA station chief said that he would have meals prepared for us to be sent to the plane and we could sleep on the aircraft. In order to pass the time until dinner, we went to the International lounge and had a soft drink (absolutely no booze in Libya).

Well, my partner said something about me having a bottle of Johnnie Walker Red on the plane and the bartender—overhearing our conversation—insisted that I sell it to him at a good price. I said, "Hey, your government wonon't let us into the country and now You want to buy Scotch from me-an act that probably would put all of us in jail. No way He may have very well been a set up—who knows? To top it off, when we took our jackets off in the cabin to eat our meal, the TWA station chief saw our side arms and said he had no idea that we were armed.

I wonder how the thought we would thwart a skyjacking without them?

Sky Marshal R. G. N.:

I got on a TWA 707 flight early one morning on the continuation of a flight from the Far East to Paris via Athens and Rome. Now, I was wearing shorts, sandals, a short sleeve sports shirt and a necklace with a medal with the inscription "shalom" on it. I did not look like a CSO, right! Wrong! I should point out that I was in economy so I thought that my attire was a perfect disguise as a young student tourist.

Well, my partner and I got off in Athens and I thought that I had done a good job of concealing my true identity. Later, back in New York, I ran into another Sky Marshal who had taken my place in coach that day in Athens for the flight on to Paris. He told me that he sat next to the senior citizen who had been sitting next to me during my flight and she told him that she had been sitting next to the "Sky Marshal". Knowing of my attire, he asked what made her think that the guy was a Sky Marshal.

She told him that he was the only Gentile to get on the plane at the Tel Aviv Airport.

Sky marshal R.G.N:

TWA Had a station chief in Lisbon who fancied himself as a great expert on potential terrorists or skyjackers in the Middle East. Each time we landed in Lisbon, he would board the plane and give us a personal briefing after the other passengers had disembarked. He would give us all kinds of paperwork on suspicious individuals who might be boarding the aircraft in Portugal before it flew on to Madrid. The first time I heard this litany of horror and danger, I wondered why I was doing this job and what the chances were of transferring to only domestic flights.

There was one incident in which Sky Marshall prevented hijacking and arrested hijacker without being on the plane. An Eastern airlines flight with no Sky Marshals on board was hijacked in the air by a lone hijacker. The hijacker demanded to be taken to Cuba and threatened the crew with a weapon. The plane was a small one that did not have sufficient fuel for the flight and the hijacker agreed to let the plane land in Raleigh, North Carolina to refuel and to take on a pilot who was qualified to fly over water and land in Havana. The airline and our Headquarters found out that we had CSO team on the ground in Raleigh ready to board another flight. One of the CSOs was a former pilot and he agreed at the request of the FBI and police to go on board as the extra pilot. He boarded the plane in Raleigh as it refueled and, in his Eastern pilot uniform, Manage to get the drop on the hijacker and disarm him with no damage to the plane, crew or passengers

TO the best of my knowledge and research, there was only one flight that was hijacked while CSOs were on board the aircraft. This was an American Airlines 747 that was hijacked to Cuba with three Sky Marshals And an FBI agent on board. Somehow the hijacker got a weapon on board and grabbed a stewardess and put the gun to her head. The pilot agreed to fly the hijacker to Cuba and, to the relief of all, no one was injured. No one seemed to know exactly how it happened and what could have been done to prevent it. The opponents of the Sky Marshall program in Congress and in the airline industry quickly ceased upon the incident as proof that the program could not prevent future hijacking and that the funds used for the Sky Marshall program should be channeled into better equipment for pre-departure checks of passengers and their carry-on luggage.

Chapter 8
END OF AN ADVENTURE AND A PROGRAM

UPON COMPLETION OF my August/September flight duty in 1971, I was informed that I had been selected as a Customs Inspector for Dulles and officially turned in my CSO badge and equipment. Others were following the same course of action, and the CSOs who left were not being replaced. Fewer flights were covered and Congress officially terminated the program in June 1974. Any CSOs who had not left the that program previously were converted to Customs Patrol Officers and most were reassigned to our southern border with Mexico.

The new generation of magnetometers and x-rays were being installed in airports and ground security and pre-departure checks once again became privatized functions under the less than severe guidance of the FAA.

For the most part, this change of direction provided sufficient results.

The U. S. Government also negotiated an agreement with the Cuban government, which began to arrest and jail all hijackers from the US rather than treating them as heroes.

However air piracy had not disappeared entirely. In August of 1980, there were six hijackings in a week.

All involved individuals wishing to go to Cuba. Many of them were Cuban nationals who had previously defected and wished to return to Cuba. Since the metal detectors had made it much harder to smuggle a pistol on board, these hijackers usually had nothing but a bottle supposedly containing gasoline or a toy that they said was a bomb In one case, a bar of soap in a bag was the device used to threaten the passengers and crew.

In the mid 1980s there was a sudden outbreak of more serious hijackings in the Middle East involving the loss of American lives and funding was authorized for a small number of Sky Marshals under the control of the FAA. They were deployed only in special situations.

Sanctions were imposed on airports and countries that did not have sufficient pre-departure security or did not prosecute or return hijackers.

The use of bombs to destroy an aircraft in flight became a terrifying reality with the Unabomber's bomb on an American airlines flight in 1979. It was not successful. The horrific tragedy of Pan Flight 107's destruction over Scotland in 1988 by Libyan terrorists had more dire consequences.

Until September 11, the threat of air piracy was focused on the aircraft itself and the passengers on board. The danger posed to innocent people on the ground by a fully fueled jumbo jet had not been considered a real possibility by airline and government security personnel. However the basic conundrum had continued since 1970. How can one guarantee that someone or something that can destroy or divert the airline cannot be brought on board the aircraft?

There is no single answer to the problem. Technology alone cannot provide perfect security since a dedicated terrorist usually can find a way to go around or through the systems. As in the example of El Al, with its nearly perfect record in a world in which it is surrounded by enemies, willing and eager to sacrifice themselves, a panoply of security is needed-including face to face interviews of passengers by law enforcement professionals, computer screening of individuals including sophisticated profiling, technologically advanced screening equipment, tight airport facility security, and Sky Marshals. We had the beginning of such a system in 1971 but commercial pressures and the lack of an incident with severe loss tries of life, led to a decision to once again privatize the aircraft and airport security problem, which may have led to the disaster of September 11, 2001.

After years of seeking the one magic bullet, we have come to the hard reality that we must do everything not just one thing. It is expensive and time consuming; but the future of U S air travel will depend upon making passengers realize that flying is a safe way to t ravel. As in the case of the military fighting the last war, we need to consider the next possibility in the destruction of aircraft or their use in the on the destruction of other targets and not focus solely on what happened on September 11.

The recent incident in Africa involving surface-to-air missiles may be the most evident of the next threats. However, there are other weaknesses in the air divert security system such as the access to aircraft by raft? Unscreened ground personnel. Aircraft due to their very visibility and the impact of a crash on public security opinion will always be a prime target of terrorists, extortionists and others seeking attention to their causes, notoriety or financial rewards.

As in the case of passengers arriving into the United States, we must have the latest in risk-management techniques to facilitate the low risk and focus on the higher risk. This is not racial profiling but it is practical law enforcement profiling to remove those with the least amount of risk from the queue that the focus can be intensified on those of higher risk.

Frequent passengers who are willing to obtain an international identity card containing a chip with unique personal identifiers such as fingerprints or retina prints could be allowed to bypass some of the questioning and searches that the other passengers receive.

It makes little sense to blindly give the same degree of scrutiny to all if and when there are proven techniques to reduce the universe of suspects or unknown individuals.

Recent newspaper accounts of the resignation of air marshals and growing complaints about training, ammunition for practice and overtime pay lead one to question the management and focus of the program. Basically the job itself will quickly burn out the individuals in the program. No one can sit on planes for hours day after day without getting bored and a little discouraged about the future. It is different for flight crews who are flying the aircraft and assisting passengers. They have tasks to do on board which keep them alert and engaged in their jobs. They can talk and interact freely without worrying about divulging their true identities.

The air marshal must be as invisible as possible with no actions that might draw attention to him or her. It is like Chinese water torture to those who are in law enforcement and wish to act rather than be passive.

One can only hope that the TSA has some good psychologists on their staffs to find ways to reduce the strain and stress on individuals and their families. There should be some type of rotation to other ground duties to break the monotony of flight duty. Also it appears as if the TSA is trying to avoid paying scheduled government overtime of one and half of the hourly pay by paying a percentage of the basic salary for all overtime worked (termed Law Enforcement Incentive Pay or LEAP). This premium pay is intended to compensate Special Agents working administrative uncontrollable overtime such as when doing surveillance or undercover work. Flight times are scheduled so the government knows the hours over 40 to be worked. In the first Sky Marshal program, the Customs Service tried to do the same thing and lost a class action lawsuit to the Sky Marshals and had to pay for the hours.

All of us former CSOs had concerns about FAA being given responsibility for Sky Marshals and airport security. The creation of the new Department of Homeland Security helps to resolve some of these concerns by moving TSA into a Department with law enforcement responsibilities. Hopefully they will do a better job than in the past and that the program will not be subject to commercial or Congressional pressure.

Chapter 9
THE SKY MARSHAL ASSOCIATION

ALMOST EVERY YEAR, usually in Donovan's Bar in Queens, a small group of balding and gray-headed individuals get together for an afternoon of drinking and story telling. One unique factor identifying this group of retirees as something different is a small lapel pin looking like a flying pig. This is the annual reunion of the United States Sky Marshal Association. The number of members has been diminishing over the years but with the recent establishment of a new sky marshal program, the future may be bright for an influx of new members.

Along with the "flying pig" lapel pin and the old badges sealed in Lucite, there is even a Sky Marshal anthem penned by one of its members, Howard Coopennan,"

Seatbelts, I hate seat beats.
Wear them, it looks good. Food, tasteless,
monotonous food. Eat, It looks good.
Magazines, read them all.
Read, It looks good Talk, I'm tired of lying, Talk, it looks good.
Sleep? Fake it; Drink? Fake it; Movies,
music? Fake it Bathroom, save it.
Watch: Look: Study!
Don't stare, too obvious Watch, Look, Study' For what?

Bumps, Lumps, Bulges, Things Bumps, maybe from
a fall or a punch, Lumps, maybe from a kick or
disease, Bulges, wallets, passports, cigarettes,
Things, Weapons are things, Knives, guns,
grenades, are things I am here to stop things.
people moving back and forth Restless people.
People with enlarged bladders, People with aggravated
bowels, People with nervous stomachs, All at the same
time, moving, People moving back and forth.
Bad air: Bumpy air; Air pockets.
Bounce, Bump, Jerk, Shake!
Turbulence, Ugly, frightening turbulence Always after a meal.
Watch, Wait. Listen.
A…suspect? No-all suspects, Mothers, fathers, sisters, brothers.
White, black, red or yellow.
All shapes, all sizes, all suspects.
End is near. Seatbelts. I hate seatbelts.
No smoking! Well, I'm out anyway. End of the trip—that
is for most. I must return. One hour, two, maybe a day.
Back again. The same thing.
Watch, Look. Listen. Study Seatbelts. Time to start over again.

Legends of a Sky Marshal

This is a true story of the first Federal Sky Marshals or Customs Security Officers who flew the skies in the early 1970's to protect U.S. commercial airlines from hijacking. It is told through the eyes of the author who was one of the first of those trained by the Federal government in a crash program instituted by President Nixon after American aircraft where hijacked by Palestinian terrorists in September 1970 and flown to the Middle-East and destroyed.

The tragic events of September 11, 2001 have brought about a revival of the air marshal program under the Transportation Security Administration. If the original program had been maintained over the years, perhaps the horrific loss of life in New York, Washington and the fields of Pennsylvania could have been prevented. Tragically, the first program lasted only about three years before the politicians and the airlines decided that it was more cost effective to rely upon technology and low paid private screeners. This book offers the lessons of the past to prevent the same mistakes in the future.

This book gives details on the selection, training and operational techniques of the first U.S. sky marshals. It is both a serious and humorous story of young men and women trained for six weeks, given weapons and put on aircraft to fly to every location in the world. The author has collected the most interesting stories of his colleagues in the program and they are a mixture of sex, hours of boredom, hilarious mishaps in exotic spots around the world, And moments of pure terror when hijacking seemed to be unfolding.

This is a book appropriate for this moment in time when everyone is concerned with air security and a new program is being implemented.

The Federal Air Marshall Service Celebrates its
50th Anniversary On March 2, 2012

Left to right, John Pristole, Administrator of the Transportation Security
Administration, Mike Frederick (former CSO), Robert Bray, Director,
Office of Law Enforcement, Federal Air Marshal Service, the author and
Bill Friar (former CSO who were in the same TASOS class).

www.ingramcontent.com/pod-product-compliance
Lightning Source LLC
Chambersburg PA
CBHW031229120626
46545CB00003B/1056